Language Essentials for Teachers of Reading

Foundations

An Introduction to Language and Literacy

Deborah Glaser, Ed.D.

Louisa C. Moats, Ed.D.

Sopris West®
EDUCATIONAL SERVICES

A Cambium Learning Company

BOSTON, MA • LONGMONT, CO

11 10 09 08 2 3 4 5

ISBN 978-1-60218-609-5

Printed in the United States of America
Published and Distributed by

Sopris West®
EDUCATIONAL SERVICES

A Cambium Learning Company
4093 Specialty Place • Longmont, Colorado 80504
(303) 651-2829 • www.sopriswest.com

(163301/313/11-07)

How does copyright pertain to LETRS®?

Acknowledgments

We are indebted to all national LETRS® trainers as well as state, district, and independent LETRS users who have given us valuable feedback over the past few years. Due to their collective counsel, we present LETRS *Foundations* as a necessary adjunct to the original 12 LETRS modules.

We treasure the enthusiastic support of Toni Backstrom, LETRS Program Director at Sopris West, and the Sopris staff—including Steve Mitchell, Holly Bell, Rob Carson, Michelle LaBorde, and Karen Butler—who have helped us with all of the LETRS and TRE (*Teaching Reading Essentials*) projects.

To our husbands and children: Your patience with our professional zeal and the absences that inevitably accompany our work is never taken for granted and is appreciated beyond measure.

Finally, we extend warm thanks to all of the participants in LETRS, whose questions and feedback enable us to get better at what we do.

About the Authors

Deborah Glaser, Ph.D., has spent her career in education as both a special and general education teacher, remediation specialist in a non-profit learning center, administrator, educational consultant, author, and professional development trainer. She played a key role in the development of the *Comprehensive Literacy Plan* (1999–2002) on which Idaho's Reading Initiative was based, and she has trained thousands of teachers across the country on the foundations of learning to read and how to teach reading effectively as a national trainer for *Language Essentials for Teachers of Reading and Spelling* (LETRS).

Dr. Glaser authored the LETRS module *ParaReading: A Training Guide for Reading Tutors* as a tool to help meet the demand for establishing qualified tutors who understand the underlying reading skills that young children need and how to teach them. After obtaining her elementary education degree, she received her master's degree in special education and then completed her doctorate in curriculum and instruction from Boise State University, with an emphasis on reading instruction as it relates to school reform. Her current efforts are focused on advancing progress toward improved teacher preparation and the implementation of best reading instruction practices in the classroom.

Louisa Moats, Ed.D., has been a teacher, psychologist, researcher, graduate school faculty member, and author of many influential scientific journal articles, books, and policy papers on the topics of reading, spelling, language, and teacher preparation. She began her professional career as a neuropsychology technician and a teacher of students with learning disabilities. She earned her master's degree from Peabody College of Vanderbilt University and her doctorate in reading and human development from the Harvard Graduate School of Education.

Dr. Moats spent 15 years in private practice as a licensed psychologist in Vermont, specializing in evaluation and consultation with individuals of all ages who experienced learning problems in reading and language. She consulted with the state of California on the California Reading Initiative between 1996–1997 and then spent four years as site director of the NICHD Early Interventions Project in Washington, D.C. Her current work is focused on the improvement of teacher preparation and the dissemination of LETRS as a professional development tool.

Contents

An Overview

Chapter 1 How Children Learn to Read

Chapter 2 Oral Language, Vocabulary, and Comprehension

Chapter 3 Phoneme Awareness

Chapter 4 Phonics

Chapter 6 LETRS® *Foundations* in the Classroom

An Overview

Foundations: A Stepping Stone to LETRS®

LETRS *Foundations* is a professional development module for teachers of reading who are beginning to implement the components and principles of scientifically based reading instruction (SBRI). The module can be delivered in three days of face-to-face training or in six 3-hour sessions. *Foundations* consists of a participant manual that includes a DVD of demonstration videos from *Teaching Reading Essentials* (Moats & Farrell, 2007) and a presenter kit with PowerPoint® slides, presenter notes, *Teaching Reading Essentials* demonstration videos, and additional copies of important handouts.

Foundations is intended to be a stepping stone into the deeper, more comprehensive, and more challenging content of the 12 regular LETRS modules (Moats, 2004a–k; Moats & Sedita, 2004). (Refer to the back cover of this book for the module titles.) The LETRS modules treat in detail the topics of phonology, the structure of the English spelling system, vocabulary and comprehension instruction, and assessment. After learning with *Foundations,* teachers are more likely to enjoy and benefit from the regular LETRS modules.

Through a combination of lecture, whole- and small-group activities, video demonstrations, review sessions, and linkages to core reading program components, the following content is introduced in *Foundations*:

Chapter 1 ***How Children Learn to Read***

- Sizing up the reading problem in the United States
- Learning from reading research
- Characteristics of good readers
- Characteristics of poor readers
- Five essential components of literacy instruction
- Language "ingredients" and reading success
- Four major brain-processing systems needed to read words
- The predictable progression of reading development

Chapter 2 ***Oral Language, Vocabulary, and Comprehension***

- The many skills that contribute to comprehension
- Stimulating oral language in the classroom
- Teaching vocabulary
- Teaching comprehension

Chapter 3 ***Phoneme Awareness***

- Understanding phoneme awareness
- The purpose of phoneme awareness training
- Teaching phoneme awareness

Chapter 4 ***Phonics***

- Good readers use phonics
- A brief history of phonics instruction
- Contrasting phonics instructional approaches
- Who needs phonics, and how do we know?
- Phonics terminology
- Phonics content
- Teaching phoneme-grapheme correspondence and word recognition

Chapter 5 ***Reading Fluency***

- Defining and understanding reading fluency
- Measuring reading fluency
- Improving reading fluency in the classroom
- Monitoring student progress

Chapter 6 **LETRS** ***Foundations in the Classroom***

- Language ingredients and teaching "recipes"
- Three keys to effective teaching
- Teacher self-evaluation

The LETRS *Foundations* module incorporates six to eight video demonstrations of small-group instruction excerpted from the *Teaching Reading Essentials* (TRE; Moats & Farrell, 2007) video demonstration series. These video demonstrations can be found on the included DVD and are used both for modeling specific activities and for demonstrating explicit teaching. The complete TRE video series includes 58 demonstrations of instruction in essential components of beginning reading.

Many active-learning exercises engage *Foundations* participants in role play, hands-on practice with concepts, and opportunities to learn from—and with—peers. In addition, several exercises explicitly link *Foundations* content to the implementation of core, comprehensive reading programs that are currently in use in many classrooms.

The aim of *Foundations* is to help teachers construct a basic understanding of SBRI purposes, content, and methods. Teachers who understand why their programs incorporate specific components and activities are more likely to implement those programs with insight and enthusiasm. In addition, they are more likely to use assessment data wisely during instructional problem-solving and to differentiate children's educational needs. We have learned, however, that professional development should be continuous, long-term, coherent, and multilayered. Foundations should be followed by regular LETRS modules (Moats, 2004a–k; Moats & Sedita, 2004) on various topics, in-class coaching, training in specific programs and assessments, and data-based problem solving sessions among grade-level teams.

Foundations professional development should be led by veterans of LETRS content delivery.

What are the 12 core LETRS modules?

Language Essentials for Teachers of Reading and Spelling (LETRS) (Moats, 2004a–k; Moats & Sedita, 2004) is a series of 12 professional development modules for teachers of reading, spelling, and writing, including general and special educators. The modules consist of printed manuals, interactive CD-ROMs, Presenter Kits, and closely related supporting products. LETRS modules are designed for delivery in day-long institutes, one day or more per module. LETRS is *not* a reading instruction program. Rather, LETRS modules prepare teachers to learn and use any well-designed reading program, and should be implemented with program-specific training. LETRS modules aim to:

- Teach in depth the theory and practice of instruction based on scientifically based reading research (SBRR).
- Foster insight into *why* specific assessment and instruction practices are effective as well as *how* to implement them.
- Engage educators in a rewarding, informative learning experience.

What content is covered in the 12 core LETRS modules?

LETRS (Moats, 2004a–k; Moats & Sedita, 2004) emphasizes the links between research and practice and the connections to language, reading, and writing. To reach *all* learners, teachers must understand how students learn to read and write, the reasons why some students fail to learn, and the instructional strategies best supported by research. LETRS provides this information. In addition, LETRS emphasizes familiarity with English language structures that are the basis for reading, spelling, writing, and oral-language instruction. The American Federation of Teachers' *Teaching Reading* Is *Rocket Science* (Moats, 1999), the Learning First Alliance's (2000) *Every Child Reading: A Professional Development Guide*, and the Reading First Leadership Academy (2002) provided blueprints for the content that was incorporated into LETRS.

The 12 LETRS modules (Moats, 2004a–k; Moats & Sedita, 2004) address each essential component of reading instruction—**phoneme awareness**; **phonics, decoding, spelling, and word study**; **oral language development**; **vocabulary**; **reading fluency**; **comprehension**; and **writing**—and the foundational concepts that link these components. The characteristics and needs of English language learners (ELL), dialect speakers, and students with other learning differences are addressed throughout LETRS. A supplementary LETRS module (Arguelles & Baker, in press) focuses solely on principles of teaching ELL students. Instruction in assessment and evaluation of student performance is included, with an emphasis on screening for prevention and early intervention in Modules 8 and 12. The format of instruction in LETRS allows for deep learning and reflection beyond the brief once-over treatment that these literacy components are often given.

Supplementary LETRS Materials

- **LETRS Presenter's Kits** (Tolman & Moats, 2004a–b, 2005a–f, 2006a–d; Tolman, Moats, & Sedita, 2005) are available for each LETRS module. These separate CD-ROM format kits include PowerPoint slides with presenter notes, templates for overhead transparencies, handouts, general advice, presentation tips, and supplementary videos where needed.
- **LETRS Interactive CD-ROM modules** (Moats, 2004b–d and g–h) were developed with a grant from the Small Business Innovation Research (SBIR) program of the National Institute of Child Health & Human Development (NICHD) to provide for independent study and follow-up study of Modules 2, 3, 4, 7, and 8. These CD-ROMs have been proven to help teachers apply best teaching practices when they are used within a structured coaching framework.
- *ParaReading: A Training Guide for Tutors* (Glaser, 2005) is a popular training module that is compatible with LETRS *Foundations* and the 12 LETRS modules. Other recommended LETRS-related products include:
  - *Early Childhood* LETRS (Hart Paulson, in press)
  - *Teaching Reading Essentials* (Moats & Farrell, 2007) video demonstrations of small-group intervention
  - *The Reading Coach* (Hasbrouck & Denton, 2005)
  - *The Reading Coach Presenter's Kit* (Hasbrouck, Denton, & Tolman, in press)
  - *Teaching English Language Learners: A Supplementary* LETRS *Module* (Arguelles & Baker, in press)

Who delivers LETRS?

Dr. Louisa Moats works with a small, select group of experienced national trainers who have been consultants in the development of LETRS modules. Biographical descriptions of these consultants are available on the LETRS Web site (www.LETRS.com; select "Professional Development" link).

Sopris West Educational Services also publishes guidelines for states, districts, or other affiliates that wish to implement LETRS with local and regional trainers. Affiliate sites deliver LETRS with approved trainers and with the support of Sopris West. Contact the LETRS program coordinator at 800-547-6747, ext. 126, for information.

Suggested Pacing Guide for LETRS *Foundations*

We recommend at least three days for the delivery of *Foundations*. Each training day allows for a brief carryover of the previous day's study. This carryover can be used to review information or to complete a chapter before moving on. Instructors are encouraged to post an agenda in the meeting room to help participants understand how the content will be delivered over the course of the three days.

Day 1 (*morning*): Chapter 1—How Children Learn to Read

Day 1 (*afternoon*): Chapter 2—Oral Language, Vocabulary, and Comprehension

Day 2 (*morning*): Finish Chapter 2
Chapter 3—Phoneme Awareness

Day 2 (*afternoon*): Chapter 4—Phonics

Day 3 (*morning*): Finish Chapter 4
Chapter 5—Reading Fluency

Day 3 (*afternoon*): Chapter 6—LETRS *Foundations* in the Classroom

Chapter 1

How Children Learn to Read

Learner Objectives for Chapter 1

- Consider evidence that learning to read is difficult for many children.
- Know where the research consensus on reading can be found.
- Understand that biological and environmental factors influence reading mastery.
- Describe key characteristics of good and poor readers.
- Name the five essential components of instruction.
- Explore the "ingredients" of language and how they are manifested in children's classroom behavior.
- Identify the major brain processing systems involved in reading.
- Review the progression of reading development and the terminology that scientists use for phases of early reading and spelling development.

Warm-Up Questions

How would you answer these questions?

1. How long ago did humans develop spoken language?
2. When was the first alphabet invented?
3. What proportion of the world's languages has invented a writing system?
4. When did our society start to expect that everyone would read?
5. What proportion of adults in the United States is functionally illiterate?
6. What proportion of children score "below basic" on the National Assessment of Educational Progress (NAEP) (National Center for Education Statistics [NCES], 2005)?
7. What proportion of children referred to special education has learning disabilities involving reading?
8. How early can we identify potential reading problems?
9. What are the most critical skills necessary to be a good reader?
10. What are the critical components and characteristics of an effective reading program?

Learning to Read Can Be Difficult

Reading Is Not Natural or Easy for Many Children

A once prevalent "reading myth" is that learning to read, like learning to speak and to understand spoken language, is natural. Throughout educational history, some educators have argued that children will learn to read if they are read to, surrounded by books, and have a purpose for reading. Known most recently as "whole language," this approach argued that children could figure out how to read the words if they needed to and asserted that meaning-making should be the central focus of instruction. Some children do, in fact, learn to read easily and well and seem to need very little instruction to identify and make sense of written words. But how many children have that innate ability?

Common sense, human history, and reading research contradict the idea that most children learn to read as naturally as they learn to talk. Although reading is quite effortless for some children, many others struggle to read words on a page and/or to comprehend them. The human brain has evolved over hundreds of thousands of years to support the development of spoken language, and humans have been communicating with spoken language for at least 100,000 years. Written language, on the other hand, has been in existence for only 12,000 to 15,000 years—not enough time for the human brain to evolve the functional adaptations and pathways required for reading.

The first writing systems, developed independently in several cultures, did not use alphabetic symbols like the ones in our American English writing system. They used pictograms, hieroglyphics, and other symbols, which did not represent separate speech sounds in words. Approximately only 10 percent of the world's 6,000 spoken languages have ever developed any form of written language, and only some of those languages use alphabets—written symbols that represent the separate sounds in speech. The first alphabetic writing was discovered merely 5,500 years ago on the trade routes used by Semitic tribes in Egypt. Thereafter, the Phoenicians developed a complete alphabetic writing system that evolved into the Greek and Roman alphabets. Modern American English spelling, and even the use of some letters, was not settled until Webster's dictionary was published in the mid-1800s. So, the writing system we use today has been standard for fewer than 200 years!

Keep in mind, therefore, that the human brain has not had sufficient time to evolve structures and pathways that are adapted specifically for written language processing. It should not be surprising that some of us struggle to master reading and writing—an exceedingly "unnatural" challenge for which some of us are much less suited biologically than others.

Sizing Up Reading Problems in the United States

Only recently has American society become conscious of the number of people who have trouble reading and writing and the social consequences of not learning to read well. Universal literacy—the expectation that all children should go to school and learn to read—is a very modern educational goal embraced only in the last half-century. Before that, disadvantaged children, children in minority groups, and children with learning difficulties were often encouraged to drop out of school. Expectations for the "tough to teach" were minimal. Not until the NAEP was administered for the first time in the late 1970s did policymakers begin to recognize the scope and nature of reading problems in American society. National concern about reading problems has escalated as higher levels of literacy are expected from the general workforce and as research shows how vital the ability to read is for economic and social well-being. Simply put, if students don't read well, they are less likely to succeed in life.

Did universal public education (required in the United States by the 1920s) enable all students to learn to read? Unfortunately, no. In the year 2003, approximately 22 percent of all adults in the United States were functionally illiterate (NCES, 2007)—meaning that they had trouble reading a medicine label, a technical manual, or a newspaper. According to research on dyslexia (Fletcher, Lyon, Fuchs, & Barnes, 2007), approximately 17–20 percent of the student population are at risk for serious reading problems if they do not receive effective intervention. If a student is not at the 40th percentile[1] or above on a reading test in the primary grades, the student is at risk for failing high-stakes, end-of-year achievement tests now given by most states. The NAEP (NCES, 2005) consistently finds that approximately 36–38 percent of all fourth-graders in the United States are "below basic" in reading skill. And the rate of reading failure in high-poverty, minority populations is much higher—in some populations, more than 70 percent.

Inability to read is the major reason why students are referred to special education for learning disabilities. Approximately 80–85 percent of all students classified as "learning disabled" have a primary problem with language-related reading skill. Approximately half of all exceptional children whose services are funded by special education are there for reading disabilities.

For most students, reading is acquired through effective instruction and a lot of practice reading. However, individual differences in reading skill are the norm in any classroom. Some children learn easily, but many require sustained and effective teaching over several years before they can read at adequate levels. The good news is that reading is one of the best-researched areas of education, and we know that most reading problems can be addressed through instruction.

Research Informs Instruction

It is often said that teaching is as much an art as a science. Educators tend to view research with skepticism and prefer to learn from their own experiences. Yet such a large body of research about reading has accumulated in the past three decades that we can turn to scientific evidence for answers to some critical questions:

- How do children learn to read?
- Which skills are most important, and at what phases of reading development?

[1] Percentile rank should not be confused with percentage. *Percentile rank* refers to a student's place on a distribution of ability. For example, imagine 100 students lined up in rank order on their timed running speed of a quarter-mile. If a student is at the 40th percentile, 40 students run as fast or slower than he, but 60 students are faster. The 50th percentile is average—the midpoint of any distribution.

- What causes reading difficulty in most children? At what ages?
- What practices, programs, and methods work best for: (1) most students; and (2) students with specific weaknesses?

Consensus means that so much evidence has been garnered about certain truths that almost all experts agree on them. Consensus-building takes a lot of time. Many, many studies in a field as controversial as teaching reading must be done before scientific consensus is reached. Science progresses slowly, but eventually the process leads to the building of reliable conclusions. Some of the recently published books and reports that explain this scientific consensus include:

- *Report of the National Reading Panel* (National Institute of Child Health & Human Development [NICHD], 2000)
- *Preventing Reading Difficulties in Young Children* (Snow, Burns, & Griffin, 1998)
- *The Voice of Evidence in Reading Research* (McCardle & Chhabra, 2004)
- *Psychological Science in the Public Interest* (Rayner, Foorman, Perfetti, Pesetsky, & Seidenberg, 2001)
- *Handbook of Language and Literacy* (Stone, Silliman, Ehren, & Apel, 2004)

The scientific work referred to here is not the work of any one individual or agency. It represents several thousand studies, book chapters, books, and technical reports from research funded by the National Institutes of Health, the U.S. Department of Education, private foundations, universities, and other agencies. Hundreds of investigators from many fields have been involved. Some of the studies have been conducted in other countries. Thousands of subjects have been studied overall; more than half of those have been normally progressing students. Once we understand how a good reader reads, we can then understand reading failure and how to prevent it.

A study is scientific if it investigates a well-thought-out hypothesis that builds on prior knowledge. It is conducted in such a way that another scientist could reproduce, or replicate, the results. The design of the study and the subjects of the study are carefully described so that others will know to whom the results may apply. Research methods are appropriate for the questions that are being asked in the study. The reported findings of the study are subjected to peer review—that is, they are critiqued by other experts before they are published and accepted as part of the consensus-building process.

Examples of Journals With Scientific Reading Research

- *Scientific Studies of Reading*
- *Journal of Learning Disabilities*
- *Reading and Writing*
- *Reading Research Quarterly*
- *Journal of Educational Psychology*
- *Annals of Dyslexia*
- *Contemporary Educational Psychology*
- *Developmental Psychology*

Nature and Nurture at Work

One way to approach some of the research findings about learning to read is to contemplate another acquired skill—musicianship. This exercise will help us raise and answer some critical questions about reading.

Exercise 1.1 Acquired Skill and Natural Ability

- Imagine a continuum that represents musical ability, drawn on one wall of the room you are in. At one end of the continuum of musical ability is tone deafness, inability to imitate a melody, or total lack of musical talent. At the other end is virtuosity in musical performance and/or perfect pitch.
- Judge where you fall on that continuum, and place yourself on the imaginary line. (It is quite likely that there will be a "bunch" in the middle and fewer numbers on the far ends of the continuum.)

Briefly discuss these questions with the whole group:

Do you think that you were born with your level of musical ability?

no

What roles do instruction and/or practice play in musical achievement?

Instruction teaches how to read music, practice makes performance better

Would it be reasonable to expect all students to be accomplished musicians?

No

Do reading and musical attainment have anything in common?

Both require practice to become better and both require beginning instruction

If a music instruction program were successful, would all students be at the same level?

not necessarily

If a reading program were successful, would all students be at the same reading level? Why or why not?

Again, not necessarily because our brains process at different rates and students learn in different ways.

Some Critical Points about Reading—and Musicianship

Scientific research on reading growth, reading differences, and reading instruction has enabled most reading scientists to agree on the following points:

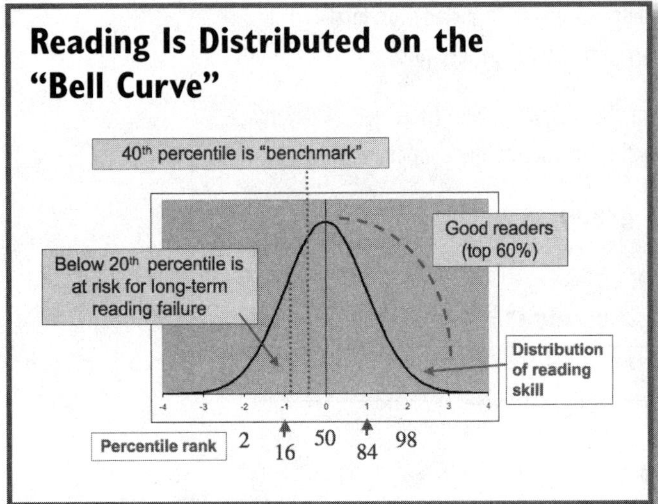

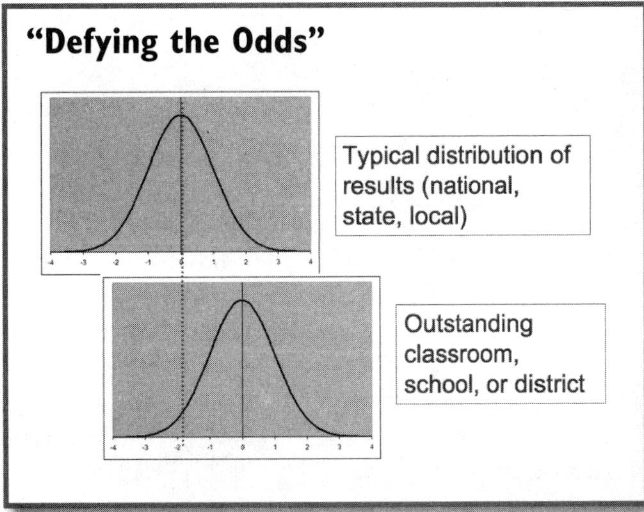

- Reading skill—like height, weight, and musicianship—is distributed on the normal, or bell, curve. Some of us seem to be born readers (or musicians), and others of us struggle. Some of that variation is due to genetics and some is due to experience, including instruction.
- If a whole-class or whole-school program is successful, the entire classroom distribution should move upward in relation to a national standard. Good readers will get better, poor readers will get better, and the class average will improve.
- Children at risk for reading failure fall behind very early in the process of learning to read. Therefore, they can be identified in kindergarten or even earlier.
- Poor readers do not catch up unless we intervene with intensive instruction. Children tend to stay where they are in the distribution of reading skill unless we give them excellent instruction. "Johnny the late bloomer" is a myth when it comes to reading ability.
- Strong early-intervention programs minimize the number of children who are going to fall behind. Success begins with early identification of children at risk. Preventive programs include excellent regular classroom instruction, small-group supplemental teaching for some students, and intensive intervention for a few students.
- Variability will still be with us if we do a good job, so flexible reading groups, peer-assisted learning strategies, multiple opportunities to practice, and well-designed centers will be needed to meet the needs of all children.

Take 2 Review

- Complete this two-column organizer.
- The first column lists restatements of main ideas. Work with the group or your partner to complete the second column by listing a few details that elaborate the main ideas or that state the relevance of those ideas to your school or classroom.

Knowledge/Main Ideas	Application/Details
1. Reading is an acquired skill.	We are not born with the knowledge of how to read. Letters need to be learned, How to recognize simple words & then longer ones, how to sound out words, etc. All takes time & practice
2. Students who are performing below the 40th percentile on primary reading tests are likely to experience long-term academic difficulty.	Be more difficult to succeed in life. So much requires ability to read - job applications are just one thing
3. Scientific research answers questions and provides a basis for developing effective reading instruction.	

Reading Depends on Many Abilities

Warm-Up Activity

(*Teaching Reading Essentials* [Moats & Farrell, 2007], Part 3, Demonstration 20. See the segment from approximately 7:00 to 12:15.)

- View a video of a child or children struggling to read with accuracy, fluency, and comprehension.
- After you watch the video, list three to five main reasons why a child might be a poor reader.

1. miss reading the word
2. guessing at new words
3. getting similar words confused
4. not paying attention to if the sentance makes sense
5. ____________________

Good Reading Requires Accurate Word Reading, Fluency, and Comprehension

What makes a good reader? Good reading depends on accurate deciphering of printed words, sufficient reading speed, and comprehension of the meaning of words, sentences, paragraphs, and longer passages.

Accurate word reading depends first on the ability to **decode** unknown words by recognizing the sounds the letters represent, and then on fast or **fluent** recognition of words that have been accurately decoded. **Decoding** is somewhat easier when words are read in the context of a passage, but a good reader can read words out of context and in lists as well as in context. A good reader typically uses **phonics** readily to sound out new words when they are encountered. Decoding skill is closely related to **phoneme awareness**, or the ability to identify the separate sounds that an alphabetic writing system represents.

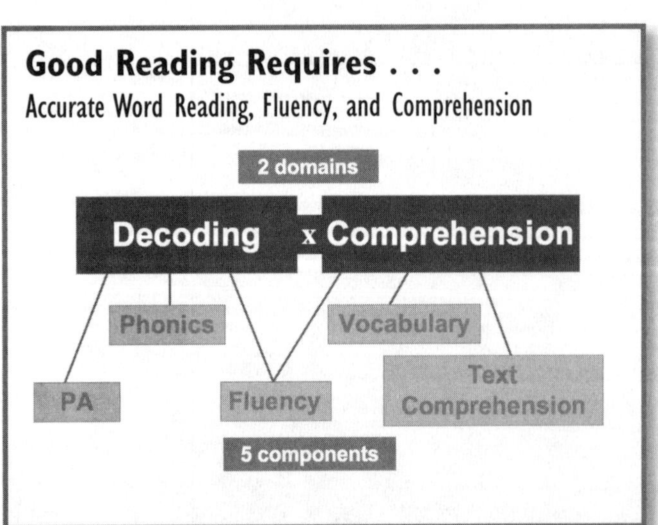

Fluency is the ability to read words, sentences, and passages with sufficient speed to support understanding. Fluency is achieved when decoding or word-recognition skills are **automatic**, or carried out without conscious attention. Fluent reading entails comprehension. A good reader sounds as if he knows what he is reading about, because he supplies phrasing and emphasis, or

prosody. Those who read fluently usually do better on reading comprehension tests and usually like to read more than students who are dysfluent or slow readers.

Comprehension is the ability to interpret the text in a way that is close to the author's intent and then to mentally integrate that information with what one already knows or has read about. Comprehension depends on vocabulary, reasoning ability, language ability, background knowledge, self-monitoring, and many subskills within these areas.

Poor reader subgroups. There are three primary causes of poor reading that have been identified by a strong research consensus (Fletcher, Lyon, Fuchs, & Barnes, 2007). Three distinguishable subgroups exist within the poor reader population, although the majority of children's reading problems represent a combination of these characteristics, and all reading problems exist on a continuum of severity.

First, the most common problem of English speakers learning in English is unremediated difficulty with phonic decoding and accurate word recognition. Those problems often originate with a specific weakness in phoneme awareness, or awareness of the sounds in speech. In contrast to good readers, poor readers are often inaccurate as they try to decipher new words because they have not learned to recognize letter-sound correspondences and/or larger chunks of words such as syllables and meaningful parts.

Second, poor reading can be caused by insufficient reading fluency. Many poor readers read too slowly. Their attention is taken up by the effort of decoding new words and they have not learned to recognize familiar words automatically. Most of the time, their knowledge of phonics and word structure is underdeveloped, and they recognize too few words by sight. In addition, weaknesses in vocabulary and overall language skill can inhibit the development of reading fluency.

Third, poor reading can occur because of poor language comprehension and limited understanding of the topic. Vocabulary knowledge and background knowledge are very important components of comprehension. A small subgroup of poor readers is able to read words accurately but not understand the meaning of passages. Most children, however, experience reading difficulties that are rooted in a combination of decoding, fluency, and comprehension issues.

Language and Literacy

Language proficiency and reading achievement are highly correlated. If students have limited language skills, they are at risk for reading problems by virtue of a developmental language disorder or by virtue of limited exposure to standard English language patterns.

Visual perception, visual-motor skills and visual-spatial reasoning are much less predictive of reading and writing skill. People who are very good at art, mechanics, dance, acting, or navigation may not be good at reading, spelling, writing, or using language. When individuals have nonverbal talents in the arts, spatial/mechanical reasoning, or athletics, those strengths may enable them to cope with reading or language difficulties, but they will still require explicit teaching of reading and language skills in order to become literate.

Many studies have reported results similar to the ones in the study summarized in the following abstract:

Summary Abstract of a Study of Language and Literacy*

[Paraphrase of original abstract]

This study examined the extent to which word reading, spelling, and comprehension are related to one another and general language competence. It also examined how teacher effectiveness and students' beginning skill levels predicted growth in reading achievement over time. The study used data from 1,342 students in 127 classrooms in grades 1 to 4 in 17 high-poverty schools. Results showed that literacy and language levels are very closely correlated in classrooms. Word-reading accuracy and fluency are very important factors in reading comprehension in the early grades. Phonological awareness predicted reading and spelling better in the early grades than in later grades. Children's language competence, including vocabulary level, perfectly predicted classroom reading achievement. Reading, spelling, and writing are very dependent on overall language proficiency.

* Mehta, P. D., Foorman, B. R., Branum-Martin, L., & Taylor, W. P. (2005). Literacy as a unidimensional multilevel construct: Validation, sources of influence, and implications in a longitudinal study in grades 1 to 4. *Scientific Studies of Reading*, 9(2), 85–116.

Five Essential Components of Literacy Instruction

Since the publication of the Report of the National Reading Panel (NICHD, 2000), most policy documents, assessment frameworks, reading programs, and teacher licensing rules have subscribed to the idea that there are "five essential components" in reading instruction programs most likely to foster success across the range of student abilities. These are based squarely on scientific studies that show a relative advantage for comprehensive programs that teach all components systematically and well. Those five essential components in instruction are:

1. **Phoneme awareness**: The ability to distinguish, produce, remember, and manipulate the individual sounds (phonemes) in spoken words.
2. **Phonics**: Knowledge of the predictable correspondences between phonemes and graphemes (i.e., the letters and letter combinations that represent phonemes) and larger chunks including syllables and meaningful parts.
3. **Reading fluency**: Reading text with sufficient speed and accuracy to support comprehension.
4. **Vocabulary**: Knowledge of the individual word meanings in a text and the concepts that those words convey.
5. **Reading comprehension**: Comprehension skills and strategies, background knowledge, and verbal reasoning are all employed by good readers to understand, remember, and communicate what has been read.

In order for reading programs to be adopted in many states and districts, thorough and informed instruction in each of these components is required, and student progress must be measured across the five components. We, the authors, believe that naming these five components was a step forward in the year 2000, and we have respected this framework in the design of our book. However, we also believe that the links between oral language and written language have been overlooked, and that more emphasis should be placed on the ways that language, reading, and writing are linked. Therefore, we move next to an exploration of language systems that are the common denominators for understanding reading and writing.

The Ingredients of Language

Language is made up of sounds, words, sentence structures, and connections among sentences. Language is heard and comprehended; formulated and spoken; read and written. When educators understand and are intimate with the many facets of oral and written language, they are better able to interpret research and to analyze and apprehend with insight the difficulties students may have. They are also more capable of understanding how children learn to read.

Exercise 1.2 Language in Cartoons

- Identify which of the following "ingredients" of language are the main source of humor in each cartoon, and list your ingredient choices on the lines provided. Because each cartoon shows language used in a social setting, they all illustrate pragmatics, syntax, and discourse. Which additional ingredients apply?

  semantics: the system of word meanings

  pragmatics: social rules about language use

  orthography: the writing system

  syntax: the system of permissible word order and sentence structures in a language

  phonology: the speech-sound system

  etymology: the origin and history of a word

  morphology: the system of meaningful parts from which words may be created

  discourse: how we combine sentences to communicate ideas

- Discuss your choices with the class or group.

____

____

____

____

"No, Daddy. I still hab it."

(continued)

Exercise 1.2 (continued)

"Mommy's spelling things on the phone 'cause Barfy's listening."

"Oooh! I learned that word in school! We better tell the police!"

"Why do I have to keep writin' in these K's when they don't make any noise anyway?"

THE FAMILY CIRCUS By Bil Keane

"Can Jason stay over? His mother works."

Exercise 1.3 Explore the "Ingredients" of Language

The goal of this exercise is to explore various parts of any language system and to become more familiar with terminology used throughout LETRS.

- **Get ready**: Make these five letter tiles and three suffix tiles on sticky notes to use in this exercise.

h	p	e	o	c	ing	ful	less

- In the first column of the table below, write your answers on the lines after the questions.
- In the second column, write the name of the language system that applies to each question and answer. (Use these language system definitions for reference.)

  semantics: the system of word meanings

  pragmatics: social rules about language use

  orthography: the writing system

  syntax: the system of permissible word order and sentence structures in a language

  phonology: the speech-sound system

  etymology: the origin and history of a word

  morphology: the system of meaningful parts from which words may be created

  discourse: how we combine sentences to communicate ideas

Refer to your tiles to complete each task.	Name the language system(s) involved.
1. **Name the letters on the letter tiles.** – Of these letters, which two never come *after* the letter **h** in English spelling? ________________	
2. **Say the speech sound(s) that each letter tile represents.** – Which of these letters represents more than one sound? ________________________	

(continued)

Exercise 1.3 (continued)

Refer to your tiles to complete each task.	Name the language system(s) involved.
3. **Arrange the first four letters to spell a real word.** ______ – Explain two ways this word is used. ______ ______ – Change the first letter to one that spells the sound /k/. – Have you made a new word? ______ – How do you know? ______ ______ ______ ______	
4. **Use tiles to spell the base word *hope*.** – Add the ending **-ing**. Write the new word. ______ – Spell the base word again. Add the ending **-ful** and write the new word. ______ – Finally, spell the base word and add the ending **-less**. Write the new word. ______ – How did you change the meaning of the base word **hope** when you changed the ending? ______ ______ ______ ______	

Exercise 1.3 (continued)

Refer to your tiles to complete each task.	Name the language system(s) involved.
5. **Use one of the words from the previous task in a short but complete sentence.** ____________________________________ ____________________________________ ____________________________________ ____________________________________	
6. **Imagine you are speaking to a discouraged student who has just experienced a loss.** – What tone of voice would you use to speak to the student about hope and/or coping?	
7. **Pretend that your class has just read a new vocabulary word, *chagrin*.** – You explain that it is pronounced *shə-grin* and that **ch** is pronounced /sh/ because the word comes from French. **Chagrin** means "distress caused by disappointment or failure."	

Reflect on the Exercise

In the second column of the following chart, note **a key aspect of student behavior** that might indicate a problem with the language system that has been named in the first column. (We include examples for the first and last language system.)

Chart of Symptoms of Difficulty With Language	
Language System	**Problem Indicators**
1. **Orthography**: knowledge of letters and the spelling system	– Student cannot remember the letters in irregularly spelled words. – Student uses impossible letter sequences (e.g., **ck** at the beginning of a word).
2. **Phonology**: awareness of speech sounds	
3. **Semantics**: knowing word meanings	

4. **Morphology**: the system of meaningful parts from which words may be created	
5. **Syntax**: the system of permissible word order and sentence structures in a language	
6. **Discourse**: how we combine sentences to communicate ideas	
7. **Pragmatics**: social rules about language use	– Student demands instead of asks. – Student does not take turns in conversation. – Student talks to adults too informally.

What the Brain Must Do to Read Words

Brain Networks That Support Reading

If reading, like speaking, were a natural skill, the brain might have evolved a specialized neural network that is employed for reading. There is no special spot in the brain that is responsible for this difficult task. Instead, several major neural systems are recruited to support reading and these must form robust connections with one another.

One system, in the front of the brain, processes the *sounds of speech*. This is the **phonological processing system**. Another system, in the back of the brain, processes the *written symbols* (i.e., printed words). This is the **orthographic processing system**. These two systems connect midway between front and back at a center where sound-symbol connections are formed and words are named.

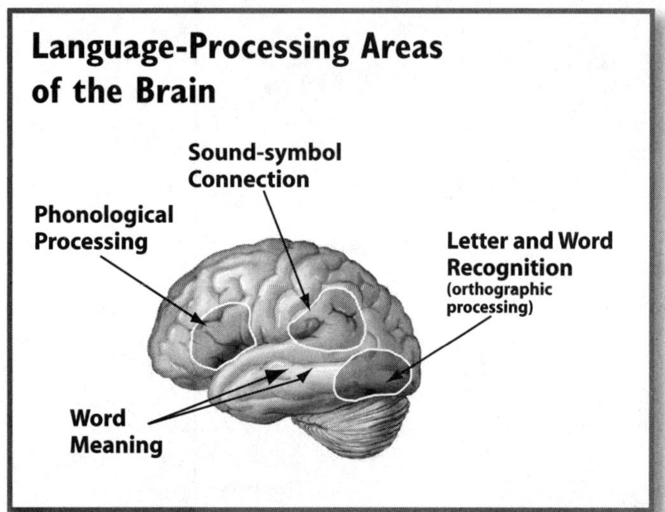

After a reader names the printed words, they are associated with **meanings**. To connect with meaning, the phonological and orthographic systems must to be "wired" into and activated with a "meaning processor" or language comprehension system. Language comprehension is processed mainly in the middle part of the left cerebral hemisphere. To process meaning, the brain must interpret individual words as well as the **context** (i.e., sentences) in which they are spoken.

The Four-Part Processing Model

The schematic diagram of the processing systems that support reading (following) represents research findings from cognitive psychology (Adams, 1990; Rayner et al., 2001; Vellutino, Tunmer, Jaccard, & Chen, 2007). It is consistent with what we have seen in studies of the brain at work (Shaywitz, 2003). The model helps us understand what is involved in the "simple" task of reading words on a page—the various reasons why reading growth might be limited.

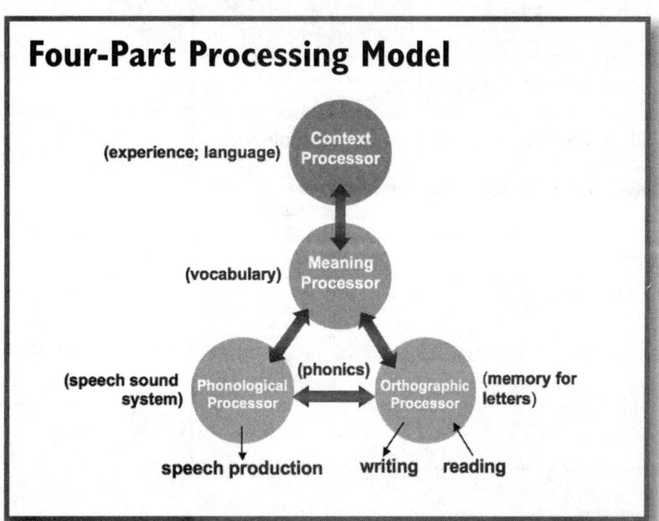

Exercise 1.4 Labeling the Four-Part Processing System for Word Recognition

- Walk through this exercise with your instructor. Fill in the correct labels for the four neural processors—**phonological**, **orthographic**, **meaning**, and **context**—in the diagram below. Briefly identify a main job of each processing system.
- After labeling each processing system, match these numbered tasks to the processor(s) that are most obviously activated while the task is performed. Place the task number inside each processor that should be activated by the described task.

1. Read the nonsense word **pem**.
2. Say the separate sounds in the *spoken* word **light**.
3. Orally give a definition of the word **unique**.
4. *Read* a sentence to determine which meaning of **pitch** is intended.
5. Determine whether the spoken words **lighten** and **lighting** end with the same speech sound.
6. Underline all the words in a paragraph that have the suffix **-ed**.
7. Write the dictated sentence "Please give me the keys."
8. Read and comprehend the sentence "The plans for the project never came to fruition."

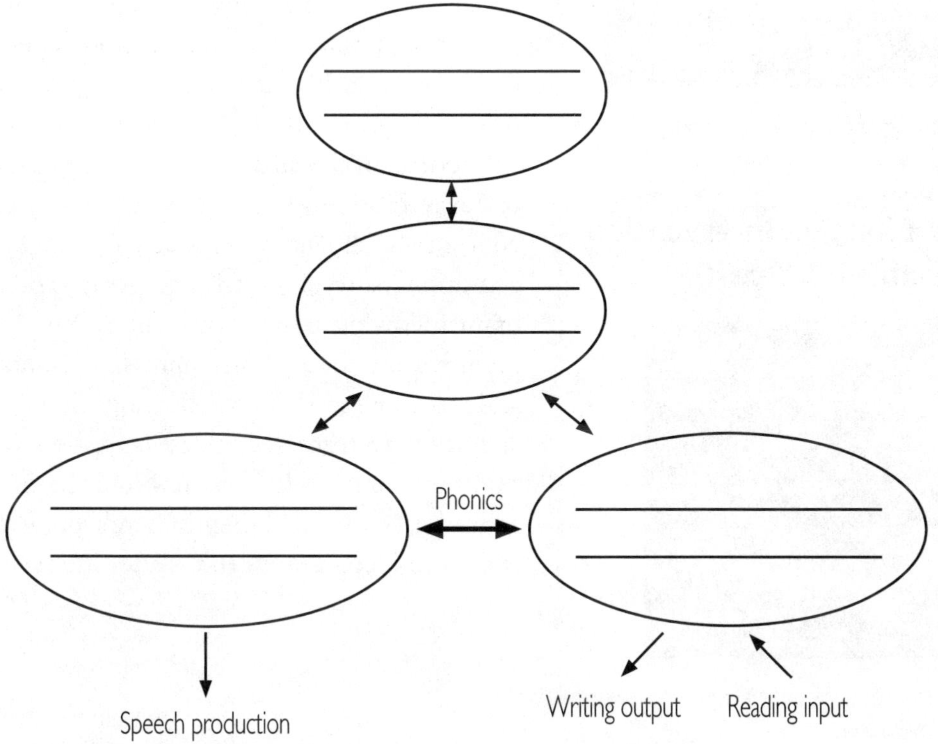

The Reading Brain at Work

The slides shown below are of functional magnetic resonance images (fMRI) of the brain at work during reading. Notice first how many areas are activated in the reading brain. Several major regions of the left brain must perform specific jobs in concert, and some activation occurs on the right side of the brain as well. Notice that the orthographic processor, specialized for storing and recognizing visual word images, is on the side of the brain (left) that serves language. Between the back (orthographic) and front (phonological) areas is an area that links phonological and orthographic information. This is activated when new words are decoded and when words are spelled. Areas that are activated to provide meaningful associations to words are more diffusely distributed in the brain.

Good summaries of recent brain studies and their implications for understanding reading and language can be found in Shaywitz (2003) and in Fletcher et al. (2007).

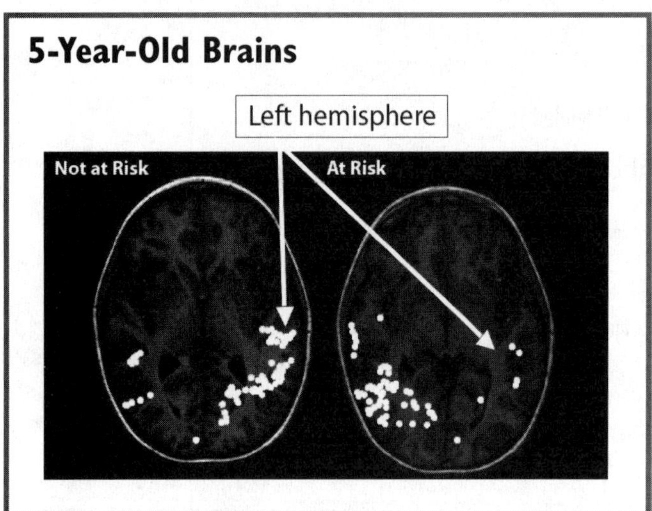

Before and After Effective Intervention for a Reading-Disabled 8-Year-Old

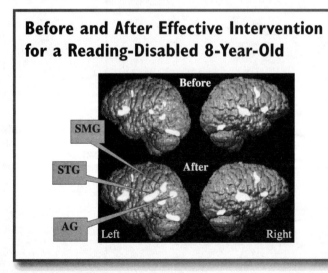

Before
SMG
STG
After
AG
Left
Right

Slides provided by P. Simos and used with permission.

First brain slide: This picture, recorded in an NICHD study, illustrates profile activation patterns in five-year-old brains for individuals not at risk and at risk for reading difficulty. The language centers contributing to reading skill are on the left side of the brain. Compare the activation patterns on the left sides of each of these brain images. What do you notice? The five-year-old who is at risk has noticeably less activation on the left side than the individual who is not at risk. The child who is not at risk shows a lot of activation in the area that processes phonological information. The at-risk child shows little activation in the phonological processing area.

Second brain slide: Studies at the University of Texas–Houston by Simos et al. (2002) provide educators with evidence for actual changes in the activation patterns of an eight-year old reader's brain following instructional intervention that is intensive and focused on improving phonological and decoding skills. Following intervention, activation patterns resembled activation patterns of a proficient reader's brain. Note the increased activation in the left hemisphere's phonological and word recognition centers after intervention.

Children Learn to Read and Spell in a Predictable Progression

Step-by-Step

The process of learning to read has been compared to the weaving of a rope from different threads or the building of a spiral staircase. Each step that is accomplished allows the next step to be accomplished. *Figure 1.1*, an image created by Hollis Scarborough (2001), shows the dynamic process by which word recognition and language comprehension subskills are combined as skilled reading is accomplished. The named subskills are like strands in a rope that become more and more amalgamated as reading skill develops.

Figure 1.1 "Rope" Model of Reading Skill Development

The Many Strands that are Woven into Skilled Reading
(Scarborough, 2001)

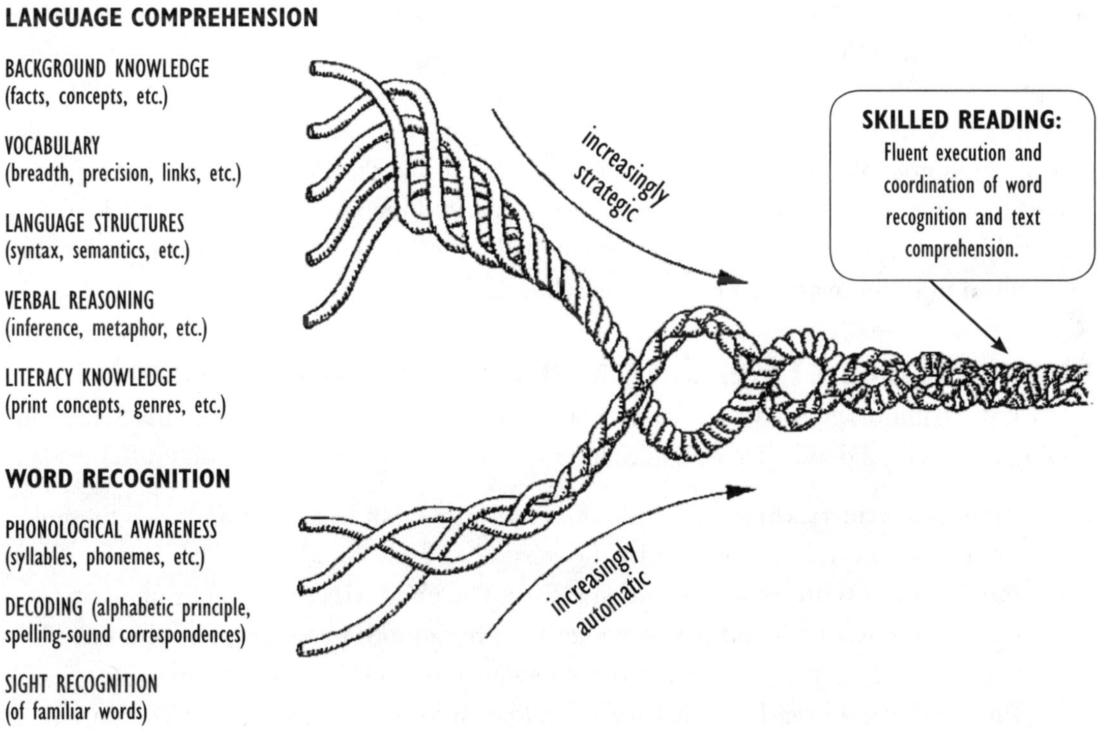

Used with permission of Hollis Scarborough.

The staircase model of reading mastery depicts a similar progression. At the base of the staircase are essential foundations for reading including recognition of letters, awareness of speech sounds, and beginning knowledge of phonics—the alphabetic principle. Knowledge of letters, sounds, and phonics allows children to recognize whole words quickly and build a sight vocabulary. Fast and accurate word recognition supports the development of reading

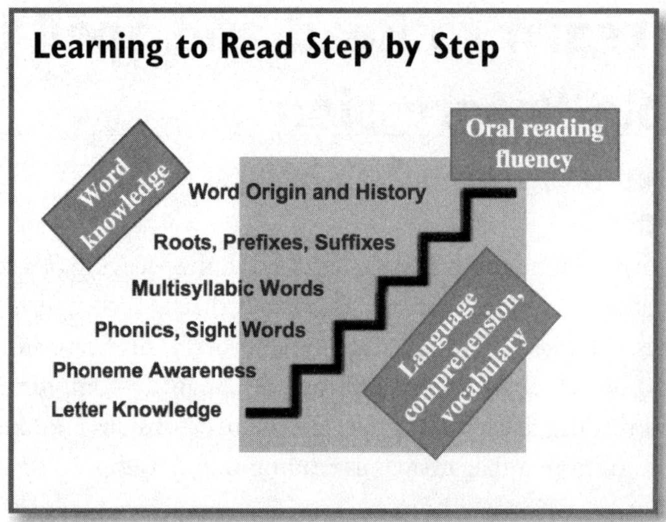

fluency. In addition, from the beginning of the learning process, language development, background knowledge, and vocabulary play essential roles. As academic language in books and in the classroom becomes more unfamiliar and demanding, those higher-level language skills become more and more important for successful reading and writing. Ultimately, verbal reasoning ability sets an upper limit on how far a person can advance in reading comprehension.

Researchers have named the phases of written-word learning, but the phases are really part of an unbroken continuum. We are deliberately avoiding the word **stage** because stages of development are not discrete. The progression of word recognition and spelling follows a predictable path, however, and has been researched extensively. The model we are following has evolved from the work of Ehri and Snowling (2004).

About Phases of Reading and Spelling Development

Current terminology used by Ehri and Snowling (2004) to describe the phases of word reading and spelling development is as follows:

- **Prealphabetic reading.** The child does not know that letters are used to represent speech sounds and cannot identify the separate speech sounds.
- **Partial alphabetic reading and spelling.** The child tries to use letter names to figure out the sounds and represents some of the sounds in a word. The child needs better phoneme awareness and more knowledge of conventional spelling.
- **Full alphabetic reading and writing.** The child has good phoneme awareness, knows most basic sound/symbol correspondences, can spell phonetically, and tries to sound words out.
- **Consolidated alphabetic reading.** The child has a substantial sight vocabulary, uses several strategies to recognize unknown words, and tries to spell the meaningful parts of words. The recognition of words is mostly automatic and attention is devoted primarily to comprehension at all levels.

Exercise 1.5 Name That Phase!

- Here are a few examples of students' written work that occupy places on a continuum of skill-level development for reading and spelling. Terms that Ehri and Snowling (2004) use to describe reading and spelling phases are listed in the second column of the chart, next to the translated examples.
- Look at writing examples #4 and #5, and decide which phase best characterizes each.
- Ask these questions as you examine the additional writing samples:
  1. Is there any indication that the student is using letters to represent sounds?
     – If "no," the student is **prealphabetic**.
     – If "yes," move to the next question.
  2. Does the student attempt to represent some of the sounds in words, using alphabetic symbols, but succeeds only with a few of the sounds?
     – If "yes," the student is in a **partial alphabetic** phase and has partial phoneme awareness and partial knowledge of letter-sound correspondence.
  3. Does the student represent all or most of the sounds in words with letters? Are some digraphs used and some irregular words spelled more or less correctly?
     – If "yes," the student is in the **full alphabetic** phase.
  4. Does the student write most words using standard letter combinations and letter sequences? Are most common irregular words spelled correctly? Are words with common endings (e.g., **-ing**, **-ed**) written correctly?
     – If "yes," the student is in the **consolidated alphabetic** phase.
- Note that phases are independent of a student's grade level.

1 PBOLRYHST	(My teacher is beautiful.)	**Prealphabetic**
There was a nit he mat a vogn the vagn floo away fam the nit the nit sed stop I am your frienb	(There was a knight. He met a dragon; the dragon flew away from the knight. The knight said, "Stop, I am your friend!")	**Partial alphabetic**
2 Once upon a time there was a nite and the nite lavde the kings dotr. Aa help me. It was the prinses a dragin kapshrd. The nite went to sav hr and he did and the prinses luvde the nite so they got mared and they livd haplale aftr. Riten and ilashtradid bi Mark.		**Full alphabetic**

(continued)

Exercise 1.5 (continued)

3	But most animals that do stay awake dering the day mostly stay in the shade. But not all animals. For example, the lizards achaly like the heat. In fact they probely couldn't live with out the heat. This is how the desert animals adapt to the desert's temperatures.		**Consolidated alphabetic**
4	I love my sistrs wisth ole my hort. I lic to pla jumup rop.	(I love my sisters with all my heart. I like to play jump rope.)	
5	. . . she belliy floped to the beach so she was todly soced so I let her use my coat. But all the ether grils bring extra close but me! So sence it was gust us grils I waked arand with gust my swim soute and swet shrite.		

Example I

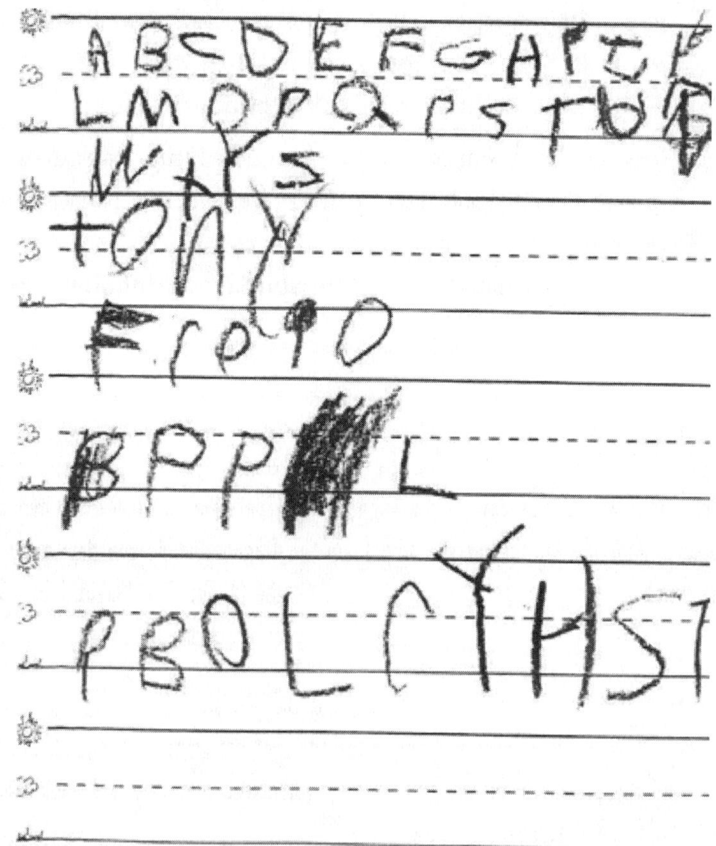

Exercise 1.5 (continued)

Example 2

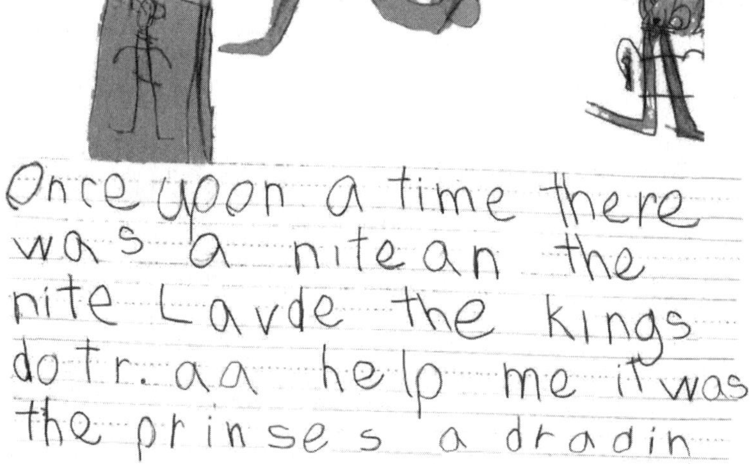
Once upon a time there
was a nite an the
nite Lavde the kings
dotr. aa help me it was
the prinses a dradin

Example 3

Since it is so hot in the desert
many animals have to find a wany to keep
cool. So the Jackrabit uses it's big ears
help them keep cool. Other animals are
nocturnal so that they are not in the Sun
so much. But most animals that do stay
a wake dering the day mostly stay
in the shade. But not all animals.
For example the lizards achaly like
the heat. In fact they probely
couldn't live with out the heat. This
is how the desert animals adapt to
the desert's temperatures.

Exercise 1.5 (continued)

Example 4

My sister I Love my Sistrs wish ole my hort. I Lic to pla Jumup rop.

Example 5

her use my coat. But all the ether grils braing extra close but me! So sence it was gust us grils I waked around with gust my swim soute and swet shrite. We got to Carolins grand parints house and the we found a 4 weler. I was the only gril how nuw how to ride one. So I hoped on in the front and Ellie in the bak grabing on to my wast. Acaly holding on for dear Life! becaus I nuw wate I was dowing (kinda) and wint around the trak mud fling up under my tiers, and wippin around the corners. Then it was some one elses turn same thing intell we count move any more cause we wear Laffing so much. We went in a hot tub, we wint on a beach and named all the Little sand bars after our selfs, we went on the 4 weller we did a lot of fun thing s on tha extravignt adventure so maby just maby if we ever stop lafing and run out of funny storys to tell maybe we will go agen.

Reflect on the Exercise

In a small group or with a partner, share your answer to this question:

- How might knowledge of the progression of reading and spelling development help you understand or plan for the students you are teaching?

____

____

____

Take 2 Review

- Complete this two-column organizer.
- In the first column are restatements of main ideas. Work with your group or a partner to complete the second column. List a few details that elaborate the main ideas or that state the relevance of those ideas for your school or classroom.

Knowledge/Main Ideas	Application/Details
1. Each of the key language ingredients plays a role in written language.	
2. The reading brain uses four distinct processing systems to read.	
3. *(Optional)* Students pass through developmental phases as they learn how oral language is represented by written language.	

Chapter Wrap-Up: Self-Evaluation

Select the statements that best identify you, and explain why you chose the statements:

- ❑ I have learned so much new information already!
- ❑ The content in this section has reinforced what I have previously learned.
- ❑ I am overwhelmed! Help!
- ❑ I have an increased curiosity about reading research.
- ❑ I want to know more about how the reading brain works.
- ❑ I did not realize how important language is to reading.
- ❑ I want to learn how to play a musical instrument!
- ❑ I want to learn how this information will help me teach reading more effectively.

With a partner, share the most exciting ideas you have had so far.

____

____

____

____

____

____

____

Postscript for Chapter 1

A few other key research findings your instructor may have time to discuss are:

- Classroom reading and language arts instruction may require up to 2.5 hours *daily* in grades 1–3 to achieve the best results with the greatest number of students.
- The emphasis of instruction will change according to grade level and students' skill levels. The balance is different at each grade level. For example, students at grade 1 may need 30–40 minutes daily of phoneme awareness and phonics, but students in grade 4 may require an average of only 20 minutes of word study per day.
- A multi-tier intervention program that includes flexible, small reading groups is desirable and supported by research. Individual tutoring is preferable and/or necessary for only a few students.
- Decisions about instructional grouping should be made on the basis of valid and reliable screening and progress monitoring assessments.
- The majority of struggling readers can be taught to read if they receive rigorous, well-designed, intensive instruction. Only 2–5 percent should experience severe reading disabilities over the duration of their schooling.

What Else Is There to Learn About Reading Ability?

LETRS *Module 1, The Challenge of Learning to Read* (Moats, 2004a) includes deeper exploration of what reading requires of the brain and how various subskills contribute to the development of skilled reading and spelling. Scientific reading research is explained and referenced. The nature of reading disability, including the definition of dyslexia, is explored. Oral and written language are compared from the standpoint of the unique demands of written, academic language on novice learners. Students' writing samples are used frequently to illustrate the phenomena discussed.

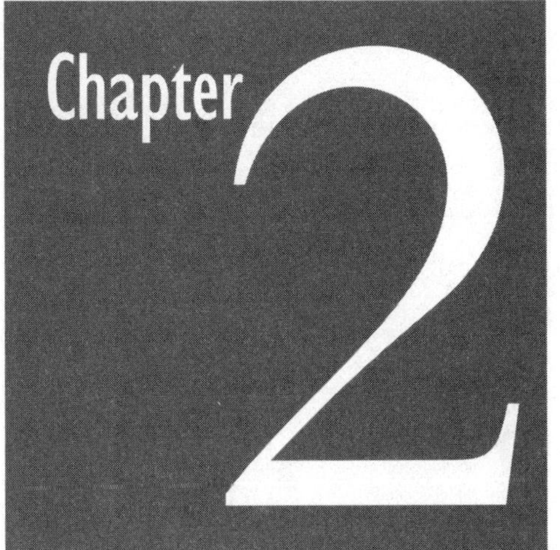

Oral Language, Vocabulary, and Comprehension

Learner Objectives for Chapter 2

- Describe the various reasons why students might not comprehend.
- Complete a graphic organizer on dimensions of comprehension.
- Brainstorm ways of increasing, stimulating, and improving conversation in classrooms.
- Design a two-minute lesson on the meaning of one new word by:
  - using it in several contexts
  - providing a student-friendly definition
  - associating it with something visible or memorable
  - showing its relationship with some other words
  - providing practice for the student(s)
- View a videotape of guided oral reading instruction and identify the strategies the teacher is using to promote comprehension.
- Practice generating open-ended or probing questions.

Warm-Up Questions

Read each of the following scenarios. Discuss *why* and *how* the following events might affect student comprehension:

1. A student is reading a passage silently and reads the word **pamper** as **pander**.
2. A student is listening to his teacher read a story and hears the word **clowns** instead of the actual word, **clouds**.
3. A student is timing himself while reading a passage. When he is through, he is glowing about his improved reading rate. His teacher asks him to tell about what he just read, and he replies, "It doesn't matter what the story was about. It only matters how fast I can read it!"
4. A student in North Dakota is reading about **beachcombing**, and she has never been to a beach or seen an ocean.
5. A student is reading a science text and does not understand the new concept that is introduced in one paragraph. She continues on, reading the next paragraph without pausing.

6. A student decodes an unfamiliar word accurately but doesn't try to figure out its meaning in the passage.
7. A student replies to an inferential question with a brief, two-word answer.
8. A student reads a complicated, lengthy sentence with an embedded clause and phrase. While he is reading the sentence, his cell phone rings.

Comprehension Involves Many Skills and Abilities

Each of the brief scenarios described in the Warm-Up embodies an important dimension of comprehension. Together, these typical classroom events begin to illustrate why comprehension depends on many different skills and abilities. Do the *sounds of language* have something to do with meaning? Yes; **clouds** and **clowns** are words that differ only in one speech sound, but diverge in meaning. Do *oral language*, *vocabulary*, *attention*, *background knowledge*, and *experience* all have an influence on comprehension? By all means. All of these variables, and others, contribute individually and in combination to listening comprehension and reading comprehension. This section provides a glimpse into these relationships and identifies a few proven classroom practices for fostering oral language, vocabulary, and comprehension abilities.

Before you begin Exercise 2.1, look back at Chapter 1 to review the list of language ingredients (see Exercise 1.2) and to review the slide illustrations that label the four neural processors that are critical for word recognition. Then, complete the graphic organizer in Exercise 2.1.

Exercise 2.1 Oral Language, Written Language, and Reading Comprehension

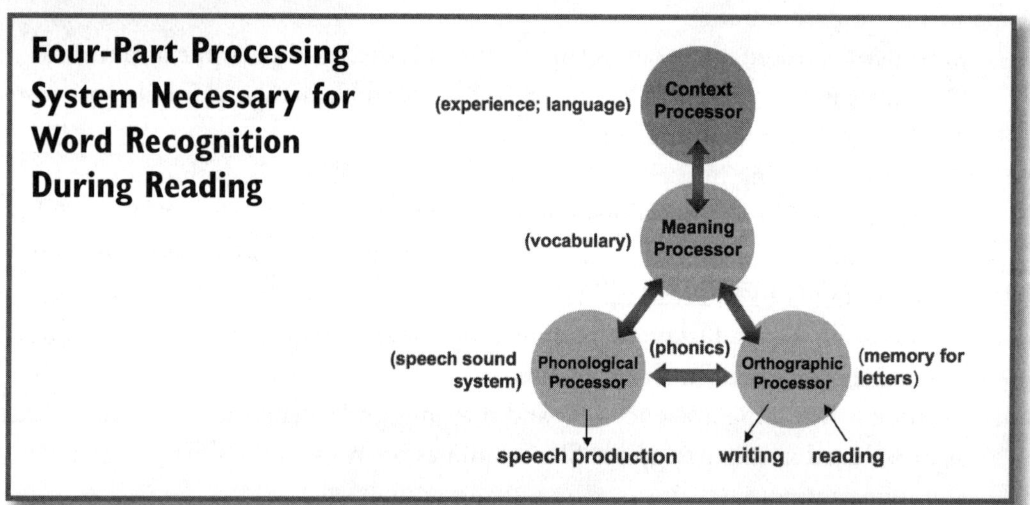

Exercise 2.1 (continued)

- How does oral language connect with written language, and how do other nonlinguistic factors combine with language to enable reading comprehension?
- Below is a simple graphic organizer depicting the interactions among these variables. Place each of the terms listed below the organizer in the blank lines under the headings you think best define them. (Some terms may apply to more than one heading.)

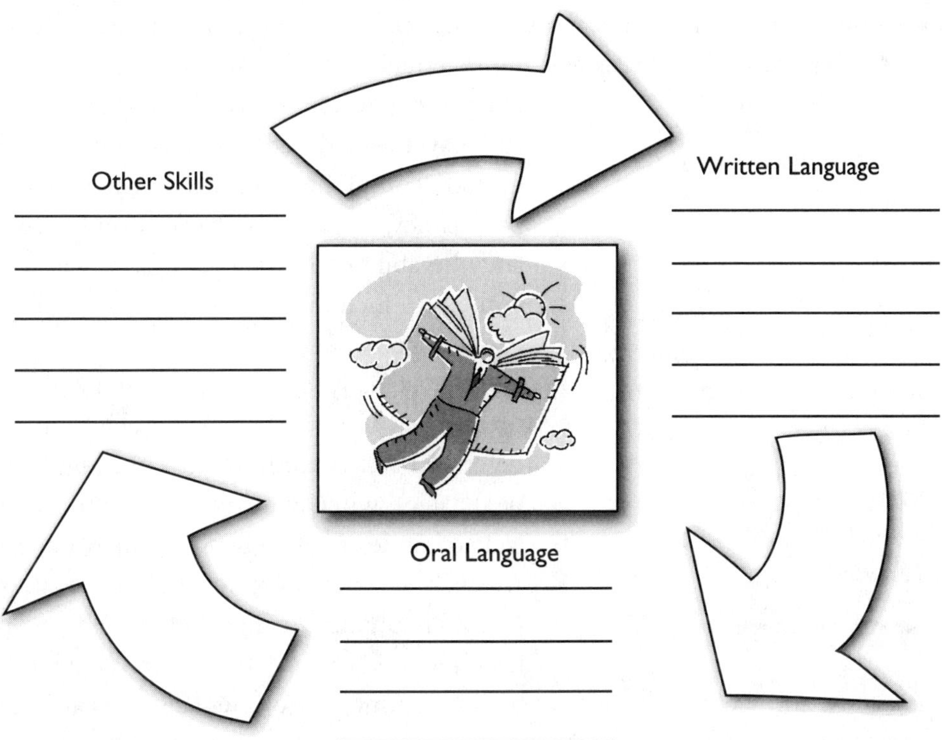

Terms for the graphic organizer: decoding, semantics, syntax, verbal reasoning, phonology, background knowledge and experience, orthography, pragmatics, morphology, attention, self-regulation, phonics, discourse comprehension, concept formation, vocabulary.

- Check your responses with the group's responses. How did you do? What have you learned about the relationships among oral language, written language, and reading comprehension?
- Now write a short paragraph that summarizes the main idea depicted by this graphic organizer.

Making Sense of the Components of Reading Comprehension

When one dissects and isolates the many skills and abilities necessary for fluent reading with comprehension, learning to read can seem like an almost impossible task! It seems even more remarkable that so many students read quite well. Not only must the basic elements of the reading process be learned, but students must also attend to the task at hand, regulate their own reading rate, and read for specific purposes (Westby, 2004). The notion that reading comprehension is very complex and multidimensional is of critical importance to educators who want to increase reading levels and improve higher-order thinking skills. Without this perspective, teachers may be influenced by fads and pay too little attention to the anchors that ground comprehension: decoding, oral language proficiency, vocabulary, background knowledge, and the ability to connect what is read to other contexts, including one's own and others' experiences.

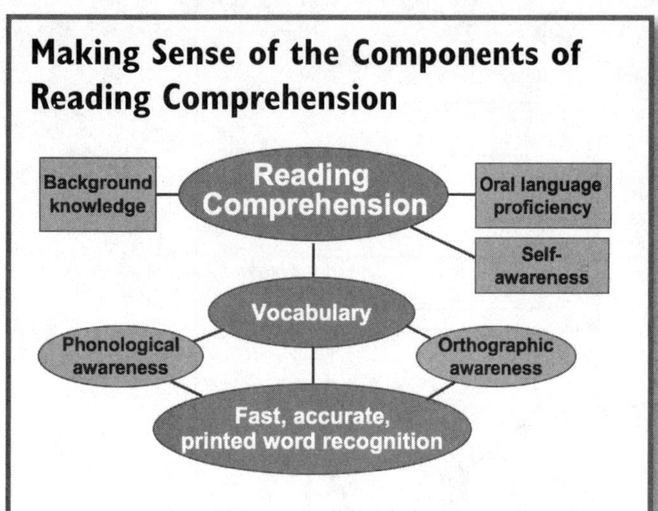

How, actually, do we make sense of written text? The processes of comprehension can be described as labyrinthine. In a reading maze (see next page), when we run into a blind alley (i.e., lack of understanding), instead of reading ahead, we seek another route through the text. Mental problem solving during reading can involve: (a) *rereading* or searching the text to *clarify*; (b) asking oneself a *question* and seeking the answer before continuing; (c) mentally *summarizing* what has been read so far; or (d) *predicting* where the text is going (Palinscar & Brown, 1984). Good readers engage in these mental habits automatically. In addition, good readers employ skills or tools for problem solving, such as: (a) knowing how to recognize a *main idea* and a *detail*; (b) knowing what to expect of certain text *genres* or organizational features; and (c) recognizing *key transition words* that signify logical relationships in the text (Williams, 2006). If we make the right turns, we'll come out of the reading maze with comprehension in place! But novice readers need a guide—a teacher—to help them learn how to navigate text.

The skills and strategies a reader knows for navigating text will determine whether he will emerge from the experience successful or whether he will become lost or stymied. Good readers generally have a better "tool kit" in the following language domains:

- **Vocabulary**. Knowledge of word meanings reflects home environment and social learning experience. Vocabulary depends greatly on exposure to language models.
- **Oral language proficiency**. Command of word form, sentence structure, and discourse are all parts of oral language. Oral language ability includes the production of words, sentences, and discourse.

- **Print knowledge**. More-advantaged children probably learned the ABCs and other features of books before kindergarten; less-advantaged children may be unfamiliar with books and print.
- **Background knowledge of the world**. Children who have been read to, talked to, and taken places typically have much more robust knowledge of many topics.
- **Self-awareness during reading**. A good reader keeps track of her comprehension and uses various "repair strategies" if comprehension breaks down.

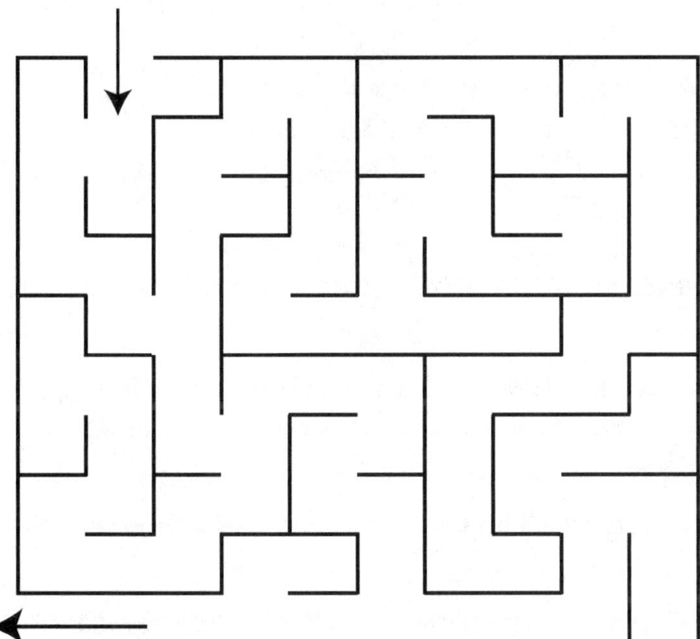

Readers experience the maze of reading by maneuvering through the turns, recognizing when the road to meaning is blocked, and retracing steps until the way becomes clear again. Reading is a labyrinthine process dependent on many strategies and skills. The teacher is a guide who leads students through the maze.

Students need teachers who will teach the skills of reading comprehension and who will build oral language, background knowledge, and vocabulary through reading aloud, discussion, and verbal modeling.

How Do Language Foundations Develop?

For the five or so years before children enter school, they develop oral language foundations that will affect them for the remainder of their lives. In the best of circumstances, children have ample opportunity to hear good language models, to interact with others, and to speak. Language is stimulated through conversation about shared experience, and language learning is by nature embedded in a social context. Caregivers' language patterns are very influential; children learn the form of language that they have been loved in. A unique and important study by Hart and Risley (1995), summarized in the following abstract, found that children from advantaged households with more highly verbal parents were far better prepared for academic learning than children from low-language or language-impoverished households.

Abstract of a Scientific Study of Language and Literacy*

The analysis of two and one-half years of data collected on the number of utterances children heard in forty-two professional, working, and low-SES families yielded many findings. By the age of three, the spoken vocabularies recorded for the *children* from professional families were larger than those recorded for the *parents* in the low-SES families. Between professional and low-SES parents, there was a difference of almost fifteen hundred words spoken per hour. Extrapolating this verbal interaction to a year, a child in a professional family would hear eleven million words; a child in a low-SES family would hear just three million. Follow-up studies at age nine showed that the large differences in the amount of children's language experience were tightly linked to large differences in child outcomes.

Detailed findings from *Meaningful Differences* (Hart & Risley, 1995) adapted from an interview with Dr. Todd Risley:

- From birth, average children heard about *fifteen hundred* words an hour addressed to them. Talkative parents exhibited the same talkative behaviors with their babies *before* the babies spoke and continued the same language behaviors when their children began to speak.
- The average four-year-old child, figuring one hundred hours a week from birth, heard *thirty million* words addressed to him/her.
- Children of talkative, college-educated, professional parents heard *forty-eight million* words addressed to them by the time they were four.
- Children in low-language, low-SES families heard *thirteen million* words addressed to them by the time they were four.
- Vocabularies of the children in poverty began and stayed relatively small and of poor quality.
- The low-SES children's parents spoke far less to them. Children heard they were right about 120 thousand times and they heard they were wrong about 250 thousand times. Their more affluent peers heard they were right about 750 thousand times and about 120 thousand times that they were wrong.
- Talkative parents produce talkative children. Reticent parents produce reticent children. When children begin to talk, they will be either talkative or reticent, depending on how much language they have been exposed to in the home.
- The relationship between the total amount of parent talk a child heard and the child's vocabulary size was .6.
- The relationship between the extra talk (talk that is above and beyond the daily business talk) was related .78 to IQ as measured by the Stanford Binet.
- All the variation in outcomes is explained by the amount of talking in the family to the babies before age three.

- The relationship between extra talk before the children were three years old was .77, with the Peabody Picture Vocabulary Test scores at age nine in the third grade.
- Vocabulary use at age three was strongly related to reading comprehension scores in third grade.

The authors of this study also concluded several years after the initial study that, given more exposure to language through conversation, children from less-advantaged homes demonstrated increased oral language abilities, vocabularies, and emergent literacy skills. Therefore, building oral language skills must be an important focus from the earliest years and throughout all of a student's educational experience.

See www.childrenofthecode.org/interviews/risley.htm for more information.

* Hart, B., & Risley, T. R. (1995). *Meaningful differences in the everyday experience of young American children.* Baltimore: Paul H. Brookes.

The "Rich Language" Classroom

The study of oral language comprises many topics, including social and cognitive factors in development, metacognition, and memory. In LETRS *Foundations*, we will focus on the development of discourse, more commonly known as the use of language in conversation and discussion. The ability to perceive, understand, store, and retrieve language at all levels develops through varied and multiple verbal exchanges with caring adults and peers. The "rich-language" classroom is one in which students are listening to new language in books and conversation, are talking to each other and to adults, are trying out new words, are expanding thoughts and observations, and are making their needs known. Quiet is not always best for learning!

Stimulating Oral Language in the Classroom

What does a classroom devoted to the development and support of oral language sound like? To begin, the teacher creates opportunities for students to listen to and use language. As with all productive teaching, the opportunities are purposeful and planned, and the techniques have been proven to demonstrate growth. Here are several methods to practice and incorporate oral language into classrooms on a daily basis.

Conversation

Conversation is a meaningful exchange between individuals that follows rules of turn-taking, listening, and responding. The goal of classroom conversation is to encourage more student talk, more peer interaction, and longer utterances. This is not as easy as it seems; anyone who has tried to pull words out of a student's mouth when the student responds minimally or not at all knows how excruciatingly difficult this can be! The teacher, more often than not, takes the easy road and ends up doing all the talking, unless he or she is determined to get students talking.

Exercise 2.2 Have a 30-second Conversation in Your Imagination

- Think of a student you know who has limited language skills. Imagine having a conversation with this student, just the two of you. Think of a question or a prompt you would use to begin a conversation on a topic you know the student is familiar with.

  ____

  ____

- Now, imagine having a 30-second conversation with that student. Your instructor will time the conversation.
- What did 30 seconds feel like? Did it seem like a long time? How much conversation could you have with that student if you allowed 30 seconds every day?
- Take 30 more seconds to tell another participant how you kept your "conversation" going with the nonverbal student.

Language-Stimulation Techniques

These four techniques are described in more detail by Lucy Hart Paulson, author of *Early Childhood LETRS* (Hart Paulson, in press) and a language-development specialist. Use these techniques to assist your low-language students to become more capable of verbal discourse!

1. **Student-oriented responses.** These are used to create and maintain a shared conversation between a student and an adult.
   Waiting: The adult uses a slow pace during conversations, listens actively to the student, and does not dominate the conversation.
   Extending: The adult repeats what the student says and adds a small amount of information.
2. **Interaction responses.** These are used to help build a student's verbal confidence.
   Pausing: The adult pauses expectantly and frequently during interactions with the student to encourage turn-taking and student participation.
   Confirming: The adult responds to the student's utterances by confirming understanding of the student's intentions.
3. **Language-modeling responses.** These are used to provide language modeling and demonstration of word meaning (vocabulary), word use and sentence structure

(morphology and syntax), and modifications of language use in social settings (pragmatics) (Justice, 2004).

Labeling: The adult provides the labels for familiar and unfamiliar objects, actions, and concepts.

"I Do, We Do, You Do": This technique is most closely related to the intentional systematic instruction that strengthens student learning. Using the simple formula of "I Do, We Do, You Do," the adult:

a. Models a concept.
b. Repeats the concept with the student.
c. Directs the student to demonstrate the concept on his own.

4. **Scaffolding strategies**. Scaffolding is a technique whereby students are encouraged to perform at slightly more complex levels over time, first with assistance and then, as they become proficient, with more independence. When instruction is scaffolded, teachers gradually release their support and feedback as students take more responsibility for task completion. The idea of scaffolding can be applied to reading and to the production of oral language in the classroom. The scaffolds are gradually removed as students gain verbal skill.

The following scaffolding strategies are used during read-alouds to increase the amount and quality of oral language that students produce. Both pictures and written text can serve as stimuli for oral language production. Read these over before starting Exercise 2.3.

Read-Aloud Literacy Scaffolds for Young Students

- **Labeling and commenting**: The teacher looks at, points to, and talks about pictures in stories.
- **Verbal dialogue about a picture or story line**: The teacher creates a story based on the pictures in a book or provides a story line.
- **Use of tag questions**: The teacher uses this type of question in conversations with students to help bridge students' understanding and to gain agreement (e.g., "That's a dog, *isn't it*? He likes red cars, *doesn't he*?").
- **Use of direct questions**: The teacher uses pointed questions to *confirm* what students understand.

Read-Aloud Literacy Scaffolds for Intermediate and Older Students

- **Pauses**: The teacher directs students to supply missing words in sentences or to anticipate what will come next. Students read along as the teacher reads the material. When critical terms and vocabulary are approached, the teacher stops and students read the word(s).
- **Reading text with syntax simplification**: When the sentence structure is too difficult for students, the teacher simplifies the story line (e.g., "The sparrows implored Peter Rabbit to exert himself" becomes "The birds told Peter to try harder").

- **Story retelling**: The teacher summarizes the story and/or encourages the student to tell the story in her own words (e.g., "Peter got stuck in the garden and almost got caught").

The next exercise involves role play of scaffolding techniques used during reading aloud (Kaderavek & Sulzby, 1998).

Exercise 2.3 Read-Aloud Scaffolding Strategies: Role Play

Scaffolding With Pictures

- Work with a partner to practice the language-stimulation strategies. Read the scaffolding techniques listed under the pictures and the book excerpts. For each technique, use the pictures and/or text to compose "teacher-talk" that is appropriate to the grade level you teach.
- Refer to the language-stimulation strategies described previously, and role-play them with a partner. Be ready to share your scaffolding techniques with the group. (Remember to follow the "I Do, We Do, You Do" procedure!)

*

Labeling and commenting: The teacher looks at, points to, and talks about pictures in stories.

Verbal dialogue about a picture or story line: The teacher creates a story based on the pictures in a book or provides a story line.

Use of tag questions: (e.g., "That's a dog, *isn't it*? He likes red cars, *doesn't he*?")

Use of direct questions: The teacher uses pointed questions to *confirm* what students understand.

* Photos by Scott Schliebe and Dave Menke, respectively/USFWS.

Exercise 2.3 (continued)

Scaffolding With Text

Excerpt from *The Call of the Wild* by Jack London:

> Buck did not read the newspapers, or he would have known that trouble was brewing, not alone for himself, but for every tide-water dog, strong of muscle and with warm, long hair, from Puget Sound to San Diego. Because men, groping in the Arctic darkness, had found a yellow metal, and because steamship and transportation companies were booming the find, thousands of men were rushing into the Northland. These men wanted dogs, and the dogs they wanted were heavy dogs, with strong muscles by which to toil, and furry coats to protect them from the frost.

Excerpt from *Little Women* by Louisa May Alcott:

> "What in the world are those girls about now?" thought Laurie, opening his sleepy eyes to take a good look, for there was something rather peculiar in the appearance of his neighbors. Each wore a large, flapping hat, a brown linen pouch slung over one shoulder, and carried a long staff. Meg had a cushion, Jo a book, Beth a basket, and Amy a portfolio. All walked quietly through the garden, out at the little back gate, and began to climb the hill that lay between the house and river.
>
> "Well, that's cool," said Laurie to himself, "to have a picnic and never ask me! They can't be going in the boat, for they haven't got the key. Perhaps they forgot it. I'll take it to them, and see what's going on."

Pauses: The teacher directs students to supply missing words in sentences or to anticipate what will come next.

Reading text with syntax simplification: When the sentence structure is too difficult for students, the teacher simplifies the story line (e.g., "The sparrows implored Peter Rabbit to exert himself" becomes "The birds told Peter to try harder").

Story retelling: The teacher summarizes the story and/or encourages the student to tell the story in her own words (e.g., "Peter got stuck in the garden and almost got caught").

Take 2 Review

- Complete this two-column organizer.
- In the first column are restatements of main ideas. Work with the group or your partner to complete the second column. List a few details that elaborate the main ideas or that state the relevance of those ideas for your school or classroom.

Knowledge/Main Ideas	Application/Details
1. Reading comprehension is a multifaceted skill.	
2. Students' oral language skills can be improved through a variety of purposeful activities involving teacher-directed discourse.	

Teaching Vocabulary in the Classroom

- During a visit to the Monterey Bay Aquarium, a father was overheard talking with his captivated four-year-old son. As they were viewing lively sea otters zipping through the water, splashing and playing with a variety of toys, the father said, "Look at that otter amusing himself with his frisbee. He is wreaking havoc with it!"
- Later the same day, while contemplating the glowing luminescence of a tank full of softly gliding jellyfish, another parent was overheard saying to her young child, "Don't touch the glass."

These two examples present divergent levels of discourse and very different use of vocabulary. If these interactions represent habits of communication, it is obvious which child is more likely to have higher levels of oral language and vocabulary. Over time, the first child will hear many more and varied words than the second child, and thus may be more likely to comprehend well during reading.

Vocabulary is defined as the words one understands and/or uses for communication. Our receptive and expressive vocabularies are usually different; most of us understand or recognize more word meanings than we use ourselves. We are not using the term vocabulary for words the child can decode or recognize in print.

If a young child says, "When we find a spider in our house, we deport him," we're likely to assume the child is bright. Vocabulary is socially and cognitively linked with intelligence. Vocabulary tests are often used by researchers as a proxy for verbal intelligence because the correlation between vocabulary and overall cognitive ability is high. Vocabulary is also linked with higher levels of phoneme awareness and decoding ability in reading and greater proficiency in passage reading comprehension (Torgesen, 2005). Because of these many connections between word knowledge and other language abilities, vocabulary has a dominant position on the radar screens of researchers and teachers. Vocabulary development leads to higher levels of reading comprehension.

Vocabulary Instruction: Implicit and Explicit

Implicit (Indirect) Teaching

A student's vocabulary grows through three distinct experiences:

1. Being in supportive environments where words are used in conversation.
2. Engaging in wide reading.
3. Learning through explicit instruction.

Students increase their vocabulary when adults who are using the oral language stimulation techniques mentioned previously (i.e., student-oriented responses, interaction responses, language-modeling responses, and scaffolding strategies) make additional efforts to include rare and unusual words. Reading itself increases exposure to words and thus enlarges vocabulary. These are forms of **implicit** teaching. Implicit teaching happens through exposure to verbal material and accounts for the learning of thousands of words (Nagy & Anderson, 1984). Additionally, reading aloud from texts that contain unusual and rare vocabulary is an essential vehicle for teaching "literate" language before students can read those words for themselves. These methods should be used in any classroom:

- **Read orally to students often, and employ dialogic reading techniques**. Choose text that provides exposure to unique and rare vocabulary. Use the vocabulary to discuss the reading selection during and after reading. Dialogic reading means that the dialogue is shared and interactive. Students are talking, too!
- **Include informational books for oral reading**. This is especially important in schools with high numbers of students who have had limited opportunities to experience and interact with the wider world and therefore may not know the vocabularies associated with those experiences.

- **Lead and promote discussions using vocabulary from the readings.** For example, ask students, "Why do you think she decided to give him the note? Use the word *frustrated* in your response." Apply new vocabulary in discussions about familiar concepts in a variety of contexts and settings.
- **Increase opportunities for students to read on their own as their reading skills and fluency rates improve.** Remember, *monitored oral reading* is preferred to silent, unmonitored reading for students who are still mastering basic reading skills. Monitored reading means that the teacher checks to ensure that the reading level is appropriate (i.e., students read with at least 90 percent accuracy). Monitoring requires listening to students read for a brief period of time and checking for comprehension.

As important as teaching vocabulary implicitly is, however, it is not enough (Beck, McKeown, & Kucan, 2002). One exposure to a word will seldom be enough to generate deep knowledge of that word. Approximately six to twelve exposures to a word in context are usually needed before students can determine a meaning, remember it, and use the word correctly (Jenkins, Stein, & Wysocki, 1984)! Additionally, students with language disabilities may require even more exposures and opportunities to use new vocabulary before the words are learned. Therefore, teachers must also provide **explicit** vocabulary instruction to enhance and increase students' vocabularies.

Explicit (Direct) Teaching

There are two main issues to consider in planning explicit vocabulary instruction: (1) which words to teach; and (2) how to get their meanings across. Each of these issues is discussed below, along with a sample vocabulary lesson and an opportunity to try out a few techniques.

Choosing Words to Teach

Preteaching selected words that students will hear and read can increase vocabulary knowledge and comprehension. Preteaching primes the pump; it alerts students to pay attention to how the words will be used in context. Choosing words for instruction, however, can be a challenging task, because there are so many words to choose from. Which ones will be best, and how many words should be taught? This dilemma has been examined by many researchers (e.g., Beck et al., 2002; Graves, 2006) who have developed a way to think about choosing the best words to teach:

- **Choose words that have *high utility*,** or words that students may not be familiar with but will encounter often and that can be applied in discussions about a variety of experiences.
- **Choose words for which students have a concept** and know another more common word with which to define the chosen word.
- **Choose three to five words per reading selection.** Depending on the age of the students and their current language levels, the number of words may increase. Beck et al. (2002) recommend setting a goal of 400 words per year.

To address the issue of which words to teach, Beck et al. (2002) have recommended that words be sorted into three tiers, or levels, as described below. The words teachers choose to teach will also depend on their students' grade level, background experience, and knowledge about the reading topics. For example, younger students and ESL students may need proportionately more instruction with Level One words. Most students, however, benefit from instruction focused on Level Two words.

Level One: Most students know these words.

- Basic, common vocabulary that children learn early (e.g., **sad**, **laugh**, **hot**).
- Important for high-risk learners and ELL/ESL students.
- Critical to the comprehension of written material.

Level Two: Highlight these words to teach explicitly.

- High-frequency, yet more sophisticated than basic words (e.g., **avoid**, **fortunate**, **industrious**).
- Can be applied to discussions across many contexts and experiences.
- Words for which students have a concept and can use a basic word to define (e.g., **fortunate** can be defined with **lucky**; **industrious** can be defined with **hardworking** or **busy**).
- Should be taught in depth; aim to teach about 400 words per year, or 12–15 words per week.

Level Three: Provide brief definition in context and move on.

- Low-occurrence words, yet critical to understanding a specific domain.
- May be particular to certain topics or fields of endeavor (e.g., **crochet**, **seam**, **bias**).
- Instruct these individual words when the need arises.

Exercise 2.4 Practice Selecting Words to Teach

- Choose one of the following three excerpts that is most representative of reading material for the grade level you teach: *Flashy Fantastic Rain Forest Frogs*, *Mr. Popper's Penguins*, or *The Hound of the Baskervilles*.
- After reading the text selection, list potential words for vocabulary instruction in the chart. Identify five Level One words and five Level Two words, and determine if there are any Level Three words. The Level Two words will be the target words for explicit instruction.
- Be ready to share your thinking for choosing and grouping the words.

(continued)

Exercise 2.4 (continued)

FLASHY FANTASTIC RAIN FOREST FROGS

By D. H. Patent

New York: Walker & Company, 1997

(Read-aloud K–grade 2, also grades 3 and 4)

The disguise of the horned frogs also protects them from becoming food for larger animals. Many small frogs protect themselves by hiding, too. Some have brown patterns that disguise them on tree trunks or among dead leaves.

Glass frogs are hard to see on green leaves. Much of their skin has no color at all. It is sometimes hard to see where the glass frog ends and the leaf begins.

A few rain forest frogs have a special way to avoid predators. They have big feet with webbing between the toes. Some also have flaps of skin on the sides of their bodies. To escape, the frog jumps in the air and spreads out its feet. The webbing and flaps act like wings and slow the frog's fall as it glides gently downward. When the frog reaches another tree, it can hang on with just one giant toe pad until it can grab with its foot.

Poison dart frogs don't need to hide or escape. They hop fearlessly about on the forest floor during the day. Their bright colors warn predators. "Don't touch me." Only a few animals can eat them, because their skin contains bitter-tasting chemicals. Some of these chemicals are very poisonous.

Level One (common words)	**Level Two** (most important words to teach in depth)	**Level Three** (specialty terms, define briefly)

Exercise 2.4 (continued)

This excerpt is from Chapter 10 of *Mr. Popper's Penguins.* Captain Cook, a penguin from the South Pole, has been sent to Mr. Popper's house as a gift by an Antarctic explorer whom Mr. Popper admires. Captain Cook seems to have adjusted to his new home and family; he has built himself a nest in the refrigerator. But suddenly, Captain Cook begins to show signs of unhappiness, sulking alone and refusing to play with the children in the house as he has before:

MR. POPPER'S PENGUINS

By Richard and Florence Atwater

New York: Little, Brown Young Readers, 1992 (originally published 1938)

(Text excerpt for grades 4–6)

"Better leave him alone, children," said Mrs. Popper. "He feels mopey, I guess."

But it was soon clear that it was something worse than mopiness that ailed Captain Cook. All day he would sit with his little white-circled eyes staring out sadly from the refrigerator. His coat had lost its lovely, glossy look; his round little stomach grew flatter every day.

He would turn away now when Mrs. Popper would offer him some canned shrimps.

One day she took his temperature. It was one hundred and four degrees.

"Well, Papa," she said, "I think you had better call the veterinary doctor. I am afraid Captain Cook is really ill."

But when the veterinary doctor came, he only shook his head. He was a very good animal doctor, and though he had never taken care of a penguin before, he knew enough about birds to see at a glance that this one was seriously ill.

"I will leave you some pills. Give him one every hour. Then you can try feeding him on sherbet and wrapping him in ice packs. But I cannot give you any encouragement because I am afraid it is a hopeless case. This kind of bird was never made for this climate, you know. I can see that you have taken good care of him, but an Antarctic penguin can't thrive in Stillwater."

Level One (common words)	**Level Two** (most important words to teach in depth)	**Level Three** (specialty terms, define briefly)

Exercise 2.4 (continued)

THE HOUND OF THE BASKERVILLES

By Arthur Conan Doyle

New York: Modern Library, 2002 (originally published 1902)

(Text excerpt for intermediate and secondary levels)

"Really, Watson, you excel yourself," said Holmes, pushing back his chair ... "I am bound to say that in all the accounts which you have been so good as to give of my own small achievements, you have habitually underrated your own abilities. It may be that you are not yourself luminous, but you are a conductor of light. Some people without possessing genius have a remarkable power of stimulating it. I confess, my dear fellow, that I am very much in your debt."

He had never said as much before, and I must admit that his words gave me keen pleasure, for I had often been piqued by his indifference to my admiration and to the attempts which I had made to give publicity to his methods. I was proud, too, to think that I had so far mastered his system as to apply it in a way which earned his approval. He now took the stick from my hands and examined it for a few minutes with his naked eyes. Then with an expression of interest he laid down his cigarette, and carrying the cane to the window, he looked over it again with a convex lens.

"Interesting, though elementary," said he as he returned to his favourite corner of the settee. "There are certainly one or two indications upon the stick. It gives us the basis for several deductions."

Level One (common words)	**Level Two** (most important words to teach in depth)	**Level Three** (specialty terms, define briefly)

Exercise 2.4 (continued)

To review:

- **Level One** are *high-frequency words.*
- **Level Two** words *deserve the greatest focus in instruction.* They are:
  - "Big Idea" words necessary to understand the central idea in a passage.
  - "Academic tool kit" words likely to be encountered across subject areas.
  - High-use words in an area of content study such as biology or history.
  - Multiple-meaning words used in a new way.
  - "Academic-discourse words" that are generally not found in everyday conversation.
- **Level Three** are specialty or domain-specific words that may not generalize across readings or appear with high frequency.

Discussion: What student characteristics did you consider when choosing and sorting your words?

____

____

____

Vocabulary: How to Get Meanings Across

Because we have such limited time to make a big impact in students' vocabulary learning, we want to make sure that the words we teach are judiciously selected and that we apply the most effective teaching methods to ensure that students are increasing their vocabulary levels. We want to teach words that will *enhance* vocabulary choices—not reiterate words that students already know—and make word-learning an all-day, everyday event! Our excitement about big words, precise words, and unusual words can transfer to and energize students as we purposefully use those new words regularly in conversation within many contexts.

Criteria for Effective Vocabulary Instruction

Apply these proven criteria for vocabulary instruction every day until they become second nature in the classroom:

- **Provide multiple exposures**. Students need at least six exposures to a word *in a variety of contexts* over time in order to learn the word.
- **Use the vocabulary words in interactive discourse**. Prompt students to use the vocabulary in their conversations with you and each other.
- **Teach vocabulary so that learning one word leads to learning many words**. Introduce words within a network of related words, synonyms, and antonyms.

Steps for Teaching a Vocabulary Word Explicitly

The following steps can be used to teach a vocabulary word explicitly. The steps provide *multiple exposures* within a setting of *interactive discourse* and introduce students to an *extended selection of words*, meeting each of the criteria just listed.

1. Use the word in several contexts, pronouncing it clearly.
2. Provide a student-friendly definition.
3. Associate the word with something visual or memorable.
4. Show the word's relationship to some other words.
5. Provide practice for students, saying and using the word.

Exercise 2.5 Part 1: Learn (and Teach) a New Word

- Experience the introduction of a new vocabulary word by your instructor. (You are playing the role of a classroom student and your instructor is playing the role of the classroom teacher.)
- Observe the application of the five teaching steps just listed, and note how these steps affect your learning of the new word.

1. ______________________________
2. ______________________________
3. ______________________________
4. ______________________________
5. ______________________________

- Complete this Four-Square as directed.

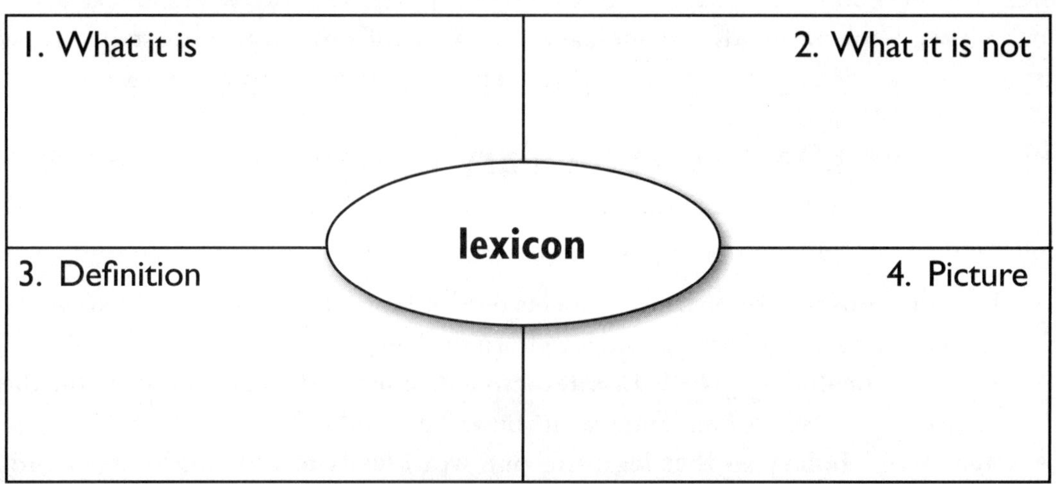

A Few Good Vocabulary-Development Activities

A variety of vocabulary practice activities should be in every teacher's tool kit. Here are a few good ones.

Four-Square

Two examples of a Four-Square are illustrated here.

1. Give students one of the Four-Square templates.
2. Working together with students, fill in the boxes—first writing the word, then adding examples and non-examples of the word, defining the word, and ending with a picture that will help students recall the meaning.
3. Talk through the different contexts students will have for the word before they choose their context and draw their picture.
4. Post the completed Four-Squares in the classroom or use them to create student dictionaries for review purposes.

1. Word	2. Examples
3. Definition	4. Picture

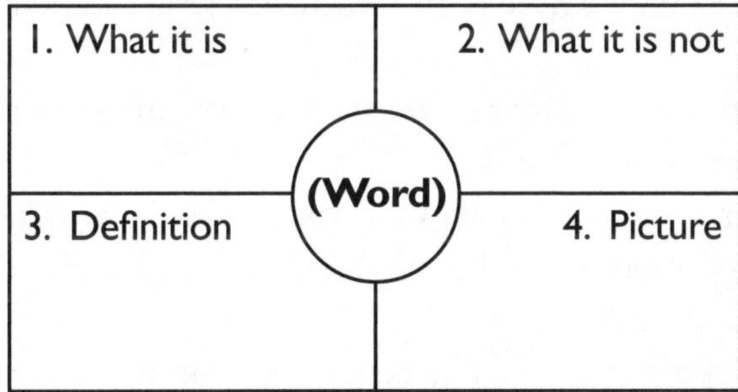

Select and Connect

This group activity is great for reviewing previously taught vocabulary and is an effective language-builder.

1. Create and display two columns of words from previous lessons on a whiteboard or chart paper. (The number of words in a column should be determined by the age of the students. Younger students are more successful if they have fewer words to choose from.)
2. Instruct students to choose a word from column 1 and a word from column 2 that can be associated with each other.

3. Ask one student to draw a line that connects the two words, and then ask him/her to explain how the two words go together. (You may need to model this step for young students.)
4. Continue by choosing two other words, and asking students to explain how the words go together. (Words can be used more than once.)
5. Continue until all words have been connected and their connections have been explained.

What words in these columns can you connect to each other? Explain your reasoning!

Column 1	Column 2
pragmatics	syntax
phonology	approval
lexicon	discourse
oral language	orthographic
semantics	vocabulary

Partner Chatter

Partner Chatter provides opportunities for students to use the new vocabulary word(s) in conversation.

1. After new vocabulary has been introduced, discussed in a variety of contexts, and after many examples have been provided, instruct students to partner up and chatter.
2. Monitor student conversations to ensure that they are using the target word(s) correctly in their conversations.
3. When you hear a good example of the word(s) being used, repeat the conversation to the class (e.g., "I just heard the word **lexicon** used to describe a very big, heavy book in our classroom!").
4. Follow Partner Chatter with a few direct questions (e.g., "Did your partner use our new word **lexicon**? Did your partner use a form of our new word **lexicon**? What words did you hear?").

Exercise 2.5 Part 2: Plan Instruction of a New Word

- Working with a partner, pick one of the Level Two words you chose from *Flashy Fantastic Rain Forest Frogs*, *Mr. Popper's Penguins*, or *The Hound of the Baskervilles*.
- Develop a routine for teaching that word, using the steps outlined here. Be ready to teach your word!

Word: ______________________________

1. Use the word in several contexts: ______________________________
2. Provide a student-friendly definition: ______________________________
3. Associate it with something visual or memorable: ______________________________
4. Show its relationship to other words: ______________________________
5. Provide practice: ______________________________
6. Teach your word to a partner!

Take 2 Review

- Complete this two-column organizer.
- In the first column are restatements of main ideas. Work with the group or your partner to complete the second column. List a few details that elaborate the main ideas or that state the relevance of those ideas for your school or classroom.

Knowledge/Main Ideas	Application/Details
1. Students learn vocabulary through implicit means.	
2. Students learn vocabulary through explicit instruction.	

More Good Vocabulary Instruction Activities

Multiple Meanings

High-frequency words often have many meanings and uses. How many meanings and uses can you think of for the word **stand**? They can be depicted in a graphic organizer, like the one below.

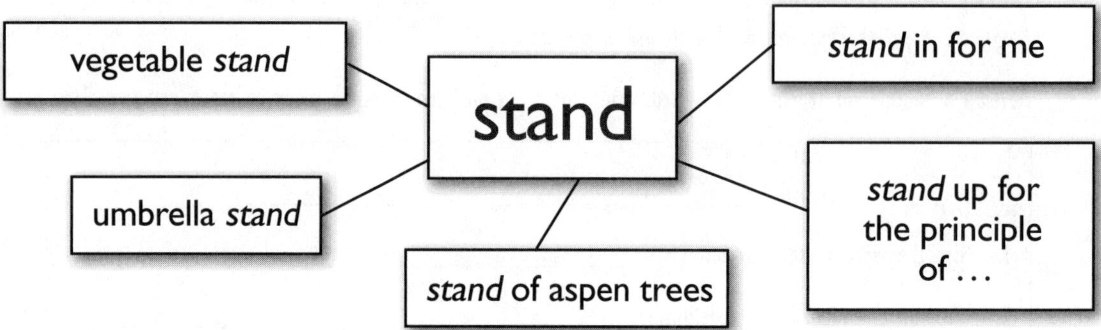

Choose one of the following multiple-meaning words—or one of your own choosing—and create another graphic organizer to show the many meanings for that word.

arm	**bug**	**chest**	**beat**	**dot**	**up**	**cross**
pan	**lift**	**row**	**sink**	**tent**	**track**	**design**

Categories

Assign the following words to one of two categories in the table: words with positive connotations or words with negative connotations.

abrupt	**important**	**corruption**	**supportive**	**disruptive**
interruption	**transport**	**corrupt**	**portable**	**rupture**
abruptly	**pandemonium**	**zoophobia**	**telephone**	**telepath**
pathogen	**anachronism**	**claustrophobic**	**psychopath**	**innovative**

Words With Positive Connotations	Words With Negative Connotations

Can you create other categories and subcategories for these vocabulary words? After doing so, sort them into the categories and subcategories you created. What do you need to know to accomplish this task? What kind of graphic organizer can you create to organize the information?

Vocabulary Note-Taking Guide

(Contributed by Kevin Feldman [personal communication, 2007] and Kate Kinsella, used with permission.)

Did you learn any new words in this section? Write them in the Note-Taking Guide below, define them, and provide an example or sentence to show you have learned the word.

Word	Definition	Example/Sentence
adaptation (n.) (**adapt**, v.)	The capacity or process of adjusting to the demands of an environment.	Birds' adaptations to extreme cold include increasing their metabolism and fluffing their feathers.
reliable (adj.) (**rely**, v.)	The quality of being dependable or able to be counted on.	Reliable friends do what they say they will do.

What Else Is There to Learn About Vocabulary?

In LETRS *Module 4, The Mighty Word: Building Vocabulary and Oral Language* (Moats, 2004d), participants learn to view words from many angles that can be exploited in instruction. Participants also explore in more detail how vocabulary and comprehension are related, and learn additional ways to explicitly teach vocabulary. Module 4 stresses the importance of semantic features, categorizing, and connecting word form with word meaning. Teachers learn how to help students create better definitions for words and become more precise in their word choice.

Teaching Reading Comprehension

Dig Into the Content

We have explored oral language and vocabulary before discussing reading comprehension for good reason. Comprehension begins with oral language and the words we know and use, so it makes sense that educators begin their study of comprehension by examining these components and how to teach them.

Preparing to teach and then leading students through the learning process can be gratifying. But how is it done? Some programs create a formula or routine for teaching comprehension strategies, but formulaic teaching may miss the point—to engage students in deep thinking about a topic or text. Regardless of the text at hand, teaching formulas such as enumerating and memorizing strategies may not serve the purpose of real engagement in meaning-making. We do not want to put *all* of our savings in the strategy bank. Not only are there multiple component skills involved in comprehension, but the most useful ones vary according to the text being read and the reader's purpose for reading. Further, once a skill or strategy has been taught, students need to be able to apply it automatically, as a habit of thinking—and focus on what is being studied. The most effective methods for teaching students how to comprehend text are those that foster active response, either written or spoken. In addition, effective teachers lead the way through the text, provide a platform for discussion, and take care to ask probing questions in an environment that encourages genuine inquiry.

An Analogy to Swimming

Let's use a familiar analogy to portray the progression of comprehension instruction. Imagine teaching a young child to swim in a lake. We begin by holding her hand and wading in the shallow water. At this stage, access to open water is limited and we are focused on establishing the child's comfort level with the water and the unknown. Reading comprehension begins the same way. The depth of text and topic exploration may be limited by the questions we ask. At a surface or beginning level, we might ask students to recognize or recall facts, definitions, and details from the text, such as, "What did the boy find under his bed?" or "How does an ant care for its baby?" We may also model or demonstrate the thought processes involved in exploration of deeper conceptual territory, as in, "It seems to me that ants always know what job they are doing. I wonder why?"

Do we want our students to stay in shallow conceptual areas? No. We want to support students, moving together into more that is unfamiliar and challenging, just as we want the swimmer to lift her feet off the bottom. If we withdraw support too fast, however, she'll have trouble. We'll release her gradually into greater depths. In the reading lesson, we'll ask questions that broaden thinking and demand better vocabulary or more analytical or evaluative reasoning. We'll probe students with "Summarize the character's experience when he was frightened" or "What were the most important things we learned about what ants need to live?" And again, we will model such skills as drawing connections between the topic at hand and our prior experience: "I think that ants do a lot of the same kinds of work that people do!"

By modeling critical thinking, skillfully querying, providing experience with text interpretation, and guiding students through text comprehension, we will enable them to read independently for varied purposes. Deeper thinking during reading and active processing of text meanings will become habits.

Three Phases of Instruction

Text reading instruction is generally planned in three phases: (a) before reading; (b) during reading; and (c) after reading. **Before reading**, we provide background information, preview the text, and help students recognize what they might already know about a topic. **During reading**, we guide students by asking good questions at critical points in the text that will help students *clarify*, *predict*, *summarize*, *locate facts*, *make inferences*, and *find main ideas*. **After reading**, we *summarize*, *retell*, and *reorganize* information, *relate it* to other readings or experience, *react* to it, or *evaluate* what was learned. None of this can happen without prior planning and establishing learning goals for our students. We have to determine where we are going before we can get there! If we clearly define our students' learning outcomes, we will more clearly lead them to that learning through our prompts and modeling.

What do you already know about comprehension instruction during these three phases of reading? Use your previous experience to supply a few good teaching ideas for each phase.

Before Reading	During Reading	After Reading

Asking the Perfect Questions

Learning to ask probing questions, or queries, that lead students to apply higher levels of thinking takes a lot of practice. Skillful questioning is one teaching skill that continues to grow and develop over time and with experience. Some teachers find it helpful to keep a list of effective question starters close by on a bookmark, with the lesson plan book, or visibly posted for quick reference. Here are some examples of those probing questions. Read through these queries. What sets them apart from simple recall questions?

- What do you suppose . . . ?
- What is the writer saying?
- What might one learn from this?
- What do you think . . . ?
- Why do you suppose . . . ?
- In what other ways . . . ?
- Tell me in your own words what [classmate] just said.
- Tell me in your own words what the author is saying.
- What is the relationship between . . . and . . . ?
- What is the writer trying to say here?
- Did the writer explain this clearly?
- Does this make sense with what the writer told us before?
- Does the writer tell us why?

Exercise 2.6 View a Video Demonstration of Guided Oral Reading

(*Teaching Reading Essentials* [Moats & Farrell, 2007], Part 5, Demonstration 5.)

- As you view the video lesson demonstration, watch for answers to the questions below.

Before Reading

1. Is a content-specific goal established prior to the lesson? Yes / No

   ____

2. Are any previewing techniques used? Yes / No

   ____

Exercise 2.6 (continued)

During Reading

1. Does the teacher help students make inferences as they read? Yes / No

____

2. Does the teacher ask probing or open-ended questions? Yes / No

____

3. Does the teacher help students make any connections to their own experiences? Yes / No

____

4. Does the teacher model or think aloud about her thought process? Yes / No
   Does she model other reasoning processing? Yes / No

____

5. Is there any misinterpretation of student responses? Yes / No

____

After Reading

1. What does the teacher do to get closure on this lesson?

____

____

Exercise 2.7 Prepare a Text for Instruction

- After you read the text selection, develop a content-specific learning goal. What learning do you want students to take away from this reading?
- Then, list two or three queries or prompts that would lead students to realize the goal.

THE FLIES AND THE HONEY-POT

An *Aesop's Fable* translated by George Fyler Townsend

New York: Globusz Publishing, 2004

A number of flies were attracted to a jar of honey which had been overturned in a housekeeper's room, and placing their feet in it, ate greedily. Their feet, however, became so smeared with the honey that they could not use their wings, nor release themselves, and were suffocated. Just as they were expiring, they exclaimed, "O foolish creatures that we are, for the sake of a little pleasure we have destroyed ourselves." Pleasure bought with pains, hurts.

Goal: ______________________________

____

____

Prompts: ______________________________

____

____

- Share your goals and prompts.

Discussion questions:

- Does your comprehensive reading program provide meaning-related comprehension goals for the reading text?
- Does it instruct you to model comprehension processes such as thinking aloud?
- Are the questions in the teacher script recall questions? Inference questions? Deeper-level prompts?
- Is there anything you need to do to improve the program's comprehension instruction?

Take 2 Review

- Complete this two-column organizer.
- In the first column are restatements of main ideas. Work with the group or your partner to complete the second column. List a few details that elaborate the main ideas or that state the relevance of those ideas for your school or classroom.

Knowledge/Main Ideas	Application/Details
1. Formulaic or strategy-laden teaching may keep us from engaging students in deep thinking about a topic or text.	
2. Comprehending text should be a scaffolded process.	

What Else Is There to Learn About Comprehension?

In LETRS *Module 6, Digging for Meaning: Teaching Text Comprehension* (Moats, 2004f) and *Module 11, Writing: A Road to Reading Comprehension* (Moats & Sedita, 2004), learn more about:

- Written language itself and the aspects of language that can be difficult for students to decipher
- The connections among phrases and sentences, the complexity of sentences, and the structures of expository and narrative texts
- Techniques for helping students construct the organization of ideas in a text and understand both narrative and expository texts
- Differences between questions and queries
- Comprehension strategies and skills proven by research

Chapter 3

Phoneme Awareness

Learner Objectives for Chapter 3

- Define phoneme awareness.
- Survey the consonant and vowel sounds of English.
- Differentiate speech sounds from letters.
- Explain the purpose and goals of phoneme awareness instruction.
- Review the principles of phoneme awareness instruction.
- Practice a few phoneme awareness activities.
- View and respond to video demonstrations of phoneme awareness instruction.

Warm-Up: Phoneme Awareness Activities

1. Divide the word **zoo** into two speech sounds. ____________
   - What is the first sound? ____________
   - What is the second sound? ____________
   - If I change **zoo** to **shoe**, how many sounds have I changed? ____________
2. Divide the word **won** into three sounds. ____________
   - Now divide **one**. ____________
   - Do these words have the same sounds? ____________
3. Listen to the sounds presented by the instructor.

   Put them together to make a word. ____________
4. Say **safe**.
   - Put the last sound first and the first sound last. What's the new word?

     ____
5. Say **light**.
   - Now say it again without the /t/.

Understanding Phoneme Awareness

What Is a Phoneme?

Spoken words are combinations of speech sounds. Speech sounds are the smallest oral language segments into which a word can be divided. For example, the word **shoe** has two phonemes (/sh/ + /ū/) and the word **stove** has four *phonemes*: /s/ /t/ /ō/ /v/. English has about 44 phonemes; some languages (such as Hawaiian) have fewer phonemes than English, and other languages (such as Thai) have many more.

Linguists define a **phoneme** as *a speech sound within a language system that can be combined with other speech sounds to make a new word.* For example, in English, the speech sound /ā/ can be combined with either /b/ or /d/ to make the words **bay** and **day**. The English words **park** and **perk** are different words because they differ in one phoneme (the middle vowel). The words **rich** and **ridge** also differ in one phoneme (the final consonant sound, which is /ch/ in the former and /j/ in the latter). We will use slashes (/ /) to denote speech sounds and to distinguish them from letters.[1]

Every language has a unique inventory of phonemes. For example, most of the speech sounds we call "short vowels" in English do not exist in Spanish, and Spanish has a different /r/ sound, a different /th/ sound, and a nasal sound /ny/ as in **piñon** or the adopted English word **canyon**. African languages sometimes include a "click" phoneme that does not exist in English. Many Asian languages distinguish vowel sounds by their vocal tone (similar to a high, medium, or low tone in singing) as well as their duration or length of pronunciation—features that English does not have.

Consonants and Vowels

Phonemes can be divided into two major groups—**vowels** and **consonants**. These terms describe speech sounds as well as letters. *Vowels* are sounds that are voiced and open; they are produced with no obstruction of the airflow through the mouth. Vowels are the heart of a spoken *syllable*; every syllable must have a vowel sound. English has about 15 vowel sounds plus the "**r**-controlled," or vowel-**r**, combinations /er/, /ar/, and /or/. (Linguists argue about exactly how many vowel sounds there are.)

Consonants are produced with obstruction of the breath by the lips, teeth, and tongue. They are "closed" sounds because the breath is closed off in some way by the articulators. The English language has about 25 consonant sounds that are represented with 21 consonant letters, singly and in combination.

Features of Phonemes

Phonemes are distinguished from each other by the placement and action of the lips, teeth, and tongue during articulation. We can describe them by describing the **features**, or characteristics, of their articulation. We can say that phonemes are *contrasted* and *identified* by their features.

---

[1] Usually, slashes are used around the phonetic symbols of the International Phonetic Alphabet. We are taking liberties with that convention.

First, a phoneme can be spoken **continuously**, until we run out of breath, like the sound /ū/ or the sound /m/, or a phoneme can be a **stop**, like the sounds /k/ and /p/. Stop sounds must be pronounced with one short push of breath.

Second, in addition to *stops* and *continuants*, phonemes are distinguished by **voicing**. Some consonants are *voiced*, and all vowels are voiced— that is, they are spoken with the voice box turned on or resonating. Some consonants are *voiceless*—spoken with the voice box turned off, like a whisper.

A third feature is **nasalization**. Nasal sounds drive the air through the nose. Most sounds in English drive the air through the throat and are non-nasal, or oral. Only three consonants in English are nasal: /n/, /m/, and /ng/.

Other important features distinguish phonemes, but a discussion of those additional characteristics will be left for Module 2 of LETRS (Moats, 2004b).

Exploring the Consonant and Vowel Sounds of English

Consonants

Each consonant sound of English has specific features or characteristics. The instructor will pronounce the underlined consonant sound(s) in each word in the table below and then ask you to repeat the pronunciation of the sound. Check the features that are true for each underlined consonant sound(s); sounds will be either *voiced* or *unvoiced*, and either *continuous* or *stop*. Alternative descriptive labels may also apply; these are supplied for you in the "Other" column. (The underlined consonant sounds in the first three words have been marked in the table as examples.) Work with a partner, if you prefer.

Consonant Sounds: Marking the Features						
Sound	Example	Voiced	Unvoiced	Continuous	Stop	Other
/b/	bat	+			+	
/p/	pat		+		+	
/m/	mat	+		+		nasal**
/t/	time					
/d/	dime					
/n/	nice					nasal**
/k/	kettle					
/g/	get					
/ng/	sing					nasal**
/f/	ferry					
/v/	very					
/th/	thistle					
/th/	this					

(continued)

Consonant Sounds: Marking the Features						
Sound	Example	Voiced	Unvoiced	Continuous	Stop	Other
/s/	Sue					
/z/	zoo					
/sh/	shoe					
/zh/	vision					
/ch/	choice					
/j/	Joyce					
/y/	yellow					glide***
/h/	hello					glide
/w/	witch					glide
/wh/*	which					glide
/l/	lunch					liquid****
/r/	ranch					liquid

* The voiceless /wh/ exists in British English but is almost lost in American English. Most of us say /w/ instead of /wh/ that spelling still indicates.

** Nasal: These phonemes require airflow through the nasal passage.

*** Glide: These phonemes glide into the vowel sound following them.

**** Liquid: These sounds float and change positions in the mouth depending on where they are in a word.

Vowels

Vowels are all open, continuous sounds. They are distinguished by the height of the tongue and by where the sound is made in the mouth. A vowel is the nucleus of every syllable; a syllable wouldn't be one without a vowel to give it life.

Pronounce the vowel sound of each underlined letter after your instructor. The category of the vowel sound has been marked for you. Note that a *diphthong* is a vowel sound that slides in the middle. Linguists often put /aw/ and /ŏŏ/ in the "Short Vowel" column, but because those sounds do not follow the same spelling conventions as the other short vowels, we put them in the "Other" column.

Vowel Sounds: Marking the Features						
Sound	Example	Short V.	Long V.	Diphthong	Vowel + r	Other
/ē/	eagle		x			
/ĭ/	itch	x				
/ā/	apron		x			
/ĕ/	etch	x				
/ă/	apple	x				
/ī/	idol		x			
/ŏ/	octopus	x				

(continued)

Vowel Sounds: Marking the Features						
Sound	Example	Short V.	Long V.	Diphthong	Vowel + r	Other
/ŭ/	up	x				
/aw/	audio					x
/ō/	over		x			
/ŏŏ/	book					x
/ū/	rude		x			
/y/ + /ū/*	music		x			
/oi/	noise			x		
/ou/	house			x		
/er/	her				x	
/ar/	far				x	
/or/	for				x	
/ə/	about					x

* The glided /y/ + /ū/ is actually two phonemes combined.

Exercise 3.1 Practice Your Sounds

- Practice saying these sounds with a partner:

  quilt /k/ /w/ /ĭ/ /l/ /t/
  box /b/ /ŏ/ /k/ /s/
  use /y/ /ū/ /z/

- Then, discuss your answers to these questions:

  1. Why would it be important for you to say the speech sounds clearly and to know the differences among them when you are teaching students to read and spell?

     ___

     ___

  2. Do these charts help you identify why students might confuse certain words or speech sounds? What features or characteristics of sounds might cause confusion?

     ___

     ___

  3. Using the sound sequence as written here for each word, count how many sounds there are in each word. Say the sounds. What is surprising about each sound sequence?

     ___

     ___

Phoneme Awareness

What Is Phoneme Awareness?

Phoneme awareness (PA) is *conscious awareness of the identity of speech sounds in words and the ability to manipulate those sounds.* PA tasks can be done in the dark, although watching the mouth of the speaker or watching one's own mouth in a mirror are helpful supports in learning to pay attention to speech. PA tasks do not require the use of printed words or letters. Once letters become involved in a task, we are probably teaching phonics, or the connections between symbols and sounds. The goal of a PA task is to increase a student's awareness of the features of speech.

Phoneme awareness is required during tasks that ask students to:

PA Task	Example
Compare or match sounds in words	Which word does not begin with /h/? **hat, hair, wind, house**
Isolate and pronounce separate speech sounds	Say the last sound in **rich**.
Put words together from their separate sounds (blending)	/sh/ /ou/ /t/ — Say it fast. (**shout**)
Break words apart into their component phonemes (segmentation)	Say the sounds in **crash**. (/k/, /r/, /ă/, /sh/)
Add, change, or delete phonemes from words (phoneme manipulation)	Say **heart**. Change /t/ to /d/. What's the new word? (**hard**)

Phoneme awareness was recognized by the National Reading Panel (NICHD, 2000) as one of five essential components of reading instruction. Approximately 25 years of research had accumulated by that time on the role of PA in learning to read, spell, and learn word meanings. Phoneme awareness is important for reading and spelling an alphabetic orthography such as English (or Russian, Greek, and Hebrew) because letters represent phonemes, albeit in a somewhat complex manner. Phoneme awareness is an important stepping-stone for beginning or novice readers and for those at any age who struggle with word reading and spelling. It is a necessary, but not sufficient, step in learning to read and spell.

Phonemes, Reading, and Spelling

Processing Systems Revisited

As we have already stated, reading words "by sight" in an alphabetic writing system involves more than simply matching a visual image in the brain to a visual image on paper. Proficient readers build a sight-recognition vocabulary by relying on several language processing systems represented in the Four-Part Processing model. All of the processing systems work together to support printed word recognition and interpretation. Best results in teaching reading (and spelling) occur when all the processing systems are addressed and connections among them are fostered. The four processing systems we described were:

1. **Context processing**—of sentence patterns, paragraphs, and the meaningful contexts in which words are used.
2. **Meaning (semantic) processing**—of word and phrase meanings.
3. **Orthographic processing**—of letters, letter sequences, and letter groups.
4. **Phonological processing**—of the sound patterns of speech, including phonemes, syllables, accent, and phrasing.

Phoneme Awareness: A Foundation for Reading and Spelling

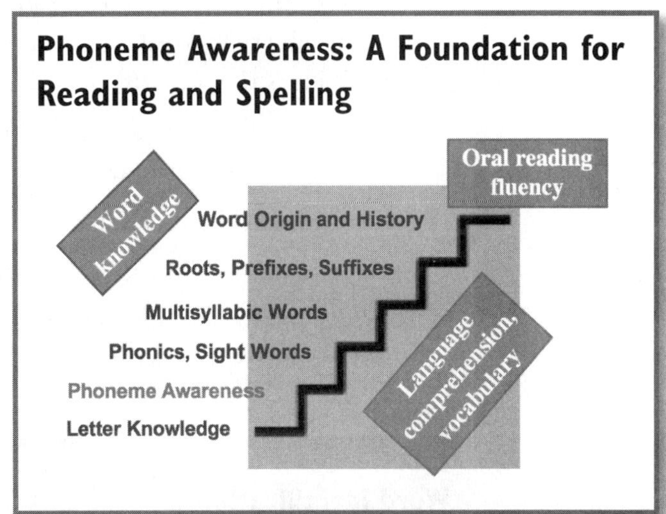

What Does the Phonological Processor Do?

The phonological processor is a brain system that is specialized for speech-sound perception and production, including phoneme awareness. It underlies or makes possible the following:

- production and pronunciation of words
- memory for the sounds of spoken language and for word pronunciations
- recognition that words do or do not fit into one's own language system
- imposition of prosody or phrasing onto spoken language
- detection of the speech sounds in words (phoneme awareness)

The Phonological Processor

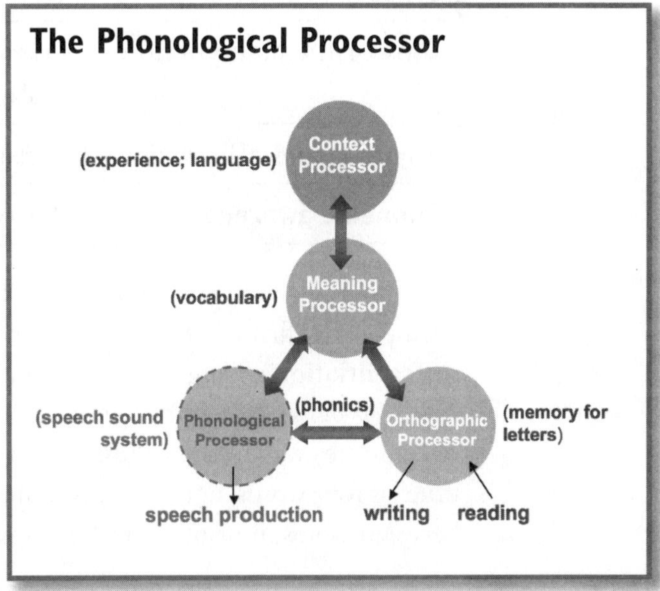

A Phonological Processing Continuum

Phonological processing, described above, encompasses a broader range of skills that go beyond phoneme awareness and that include phoneme awareness. **Phonological awareness** refers to a student's *awareness of speech and speech segments that are larger than a phoneme.* There are three sub-word linguistic units that students need to be able to identify, think about, and manipulate to demonstrate phonological awareness and to progress to phoneme awareness. These parts can be arranged in a hierarchy from easiest to most difficult:

- **Syllables**. Students should be able to segment and blend spoken *syllables* to remember, read, and compare longer words.

  ac–com–plish–ment **com–pu–ter**

- **Onset and rime**. Recognition and production of rhyming words depend, in turn, on the ability to break any syllable into two parts: the *onset* and the *rime*. The onset of a syllable is the sound(s) that comes before the vowel. The rime is the vowel and any consonants that follow it. Some words have only a rime.

  sm – art **bl – ock** **p – aste** **eat**

- **Phonemes**. The individual speech sounds that distinguish words.

  /s/ /m/ /ar/ /t/ **/ē/ /t/**

Phonological awareness, then, encompasses a wide range of skills that lead to and include phoneme awareness, as follows:

Repetition	Of sentences, phrases, or words
Word identification	Tracking or counting words in sentences
Syllable manipulation	Counting (tapping), blending, segmenting by syllable or syllable substitution
Onset-rime manipulation	Combining or substituting onsets (consonant[s] before a vowel in a syllable) with rimes (the vowel and following consonants within a syllable)
Rhyming and alliteration	Producing words that rhyme or words that follow an alliteration pattern
Phoneme awareness	Matching, isolating, blending, segmenting, deleting, substituting phonemes

Students who are not yet able to isolate a single beginning speech sound from a word, for example, may first need to attend to and differentiate larger segments of speech. **Progressive differentiation** of larger to smaller units of speech can follow a path from *syllables* to *onset-rime segments* and then to *phonemes*. But some students need to start at the most basic level of language awareness—words! For example, students need to understand that "once upon a time" is four words, not one. This skill is usually learned in preschool or kindergarten. Spaces between words in print help to demonstrate the concept of a word.

The Purpose of Phoneme Awareness Training

Phonemes—the building blocks of spoken words—are represented directly and indirectly by letters of the alphabet. Letters represent speech sounds in a complex and variable manner. Any alphabetic writing system requires a reader to associate single speech sounds or phonemes with the letter sequences we use to spell words. Children who understand that letters correspond to speech sounds have learned the **alphabetic principle**, even if they don't know all the complexities of reading.

Good readers and spellers are able to identify, separate, and blend the single phonemes in words well enough to understand how letters represent those sounds. In addition, good perception of, and memory for, the sounds that make up words is essential for associating pronunciation with meaning. If a speaker cannot pronounce a new word accurately, he might attach the wrong meaning to the word—or at least confuse the listener. Have you ever known anyone who confused **tenet** and **tenant**, or **flush** and **flesh**, for example? Those words differ in only one phoneme.

Many research studies have shown that students who are poor readers and spellers and students who are having difficulty learning phonics usually lack sufficient phoneme awareness. These students benefit from being taught the identity of speech sounds in the language they are studying, and they benefit from direct instruction in the manipulation of those sounds. Students who are taught to be aware of phonemes are more likely to respond well to the phonics component of a classroom reading instruction program.

When measured alongside letter-naming and vocabulary, phoneme awareness is an excellent predictor of later reading skill.

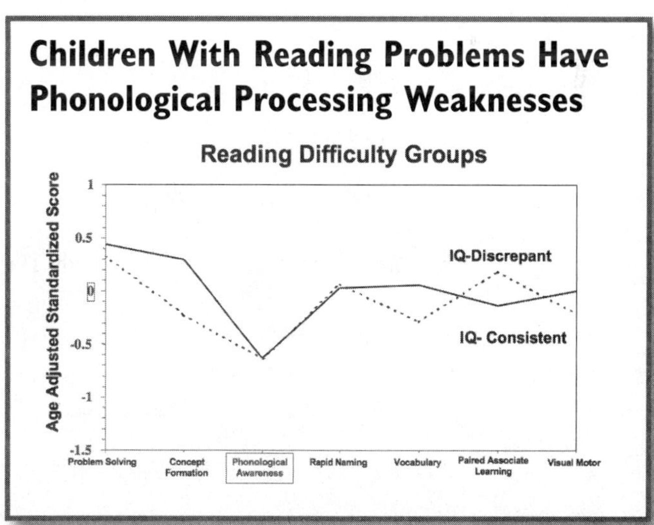

Data from the Connecticut Longitudinal Study showing relative weaknesses of 2nd and 3rd grade, reading delayed children on a range of cognitive tests, after pp. 46-56 in Fletcher et al. (2007). Slide provided by Dr. Fletcher and used with permission.

Exercise 3.2 Practicing Phoneme Awareness Activities

- Follow your instructor through these activities. Be sure to say the words out loud and feel what your mouth is doing as you articulate the sounds in each word.

1. Match the phonemes.
   - Read the first word in each row and isolate the sound that is represented by the underlined letter(s).
   - Then, circle the word(s) in the row that contain the same sound.

does	rose	miss	race	box
helped	find	rowed	past	freed
gem	get	fog	girl	bridge
sang	name	lanky	strange	pencil
laugh	faun	train	sauce	grab

2. Count the phonemes.
   - Stretch out a finger as you say each sound in the words below.
   - Write the number of phonemes on the line after the word. (The first one has been done for you.)

shoe (2)	buzz ____	slack ____	dream ____	void ____
mound ____	her ____	amaze ____	breath ____	eye ____
wheel ____	use ____	ditch ____	long ____	blank ____

3. What sound does each word end with? (The first one has been done for you.)

bathe /th/	rise ____	rice ____	rhyme ____	ring ____
fix ____	beige ____	sledge ____	winged ____	apostrophe ____

Exercise 3.2 (continued)

4. Match the sounds.

   – List three words that have the same *sound* as the underlined sound in the following words. (The sound can be at the beginning, middle, or end.) List at least one word with a different spelling. (The first one has been done for you.)

   quiet (sound = /k/): king, chorus, catch

   oyster: ____________ ____________ ____________

   machine: ____________ ____________ ____________

   irksome: ____________ ____________ ____________

   fool: ____________ ____________ ____________

5. Use sound boxes.

   – As you segment each word in the first column, put a marker in a box for each sound you hear.

   – Add the number of markers, and write the number in the last column. (The first one has been done for you.)

   – Then, practice saying the word sounds with a partner and make sure that you agree on the number of sounds.

moose	○	○	○				3
robot							
shred							
hex							
quaint							
itch							
through							
weight							
scrimp							
save							

When Do We Teach Letters and Concepts of Print?

In parallel with language development and phonological awareness, students need to learn the letter forms, letter names, and letter sequence of the alphabet. Knowing letter names is one of the best single predictors of later success in reading. Daily practice with manipulative materials supports development of letter knowledge.Young students should become accurate and fluent in letter recognition and letter naming. This is achieved through ample, varied practice with letter matching and sequencing. Learning to write letters correctly is an important component of letter instruction. A good beginning reading program will include a strand that teaches letter identification, matching, naming and copying, along with phoneme awareness. As these skills develop, students are ready for sound-symbol matching, phonics, and reading itself.

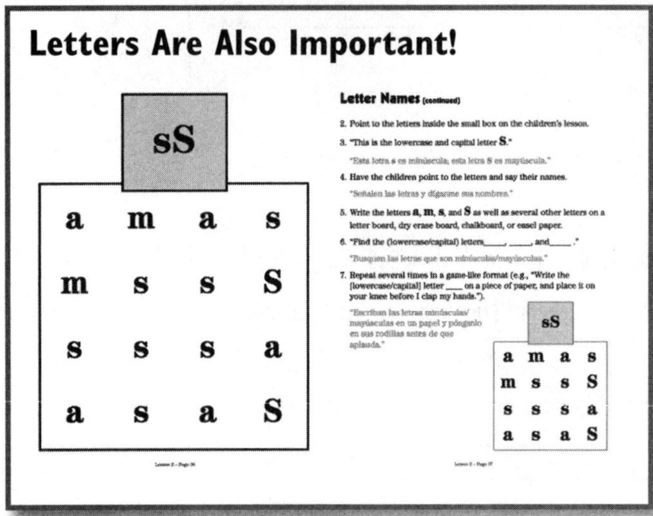

Letters Are Also Important!

sS

a	m	a	s
m	s	s	S
s	s	s	a
a	s	a	S

Letter Names (continued)

2. Point to the letters inside the small box on the children's lesson.
3. "This is the lowercase and capital letter **S**."

   "Esta letra s es minúscula; esta letra S es mayúscula."
4. Have the children point to the letters and say their names.

   "Señalen las letras y díganme sus nombres."
5. Write the letters **a**, **m**, **s**, and **S** as well as several other letters on a letter board, dry erase board, chalkboard, or easel paper.
6. "Find the (lowercase/capital) letters_____, _____, and_____."

   "Busquen las letras que son minúsculas/mayúsculas."
7. Repeat several times in a game-like format (e.g., "Write the [lowercase/capital] letter ____ on a piece of paper, and place it on your knee before I clap my hands.").

   "Escriban las letras minúsculas/mayúsculas en un papel y pónganlo en sus rodillas antes de que aplauda."

sS

a	m	a	s
m	s	s	S
s	s	s	a
a	s	a	S

Excerpted from *Stepping Stones to Literacy* (Nelson et al., 2004).

In addition, many students come to school without much experience with books. Print awareness activities are designed to teach students about the format of books, conventions such as left-to-right progression, the significance of spaces between words, and the expectation that the words should make sense. Many students must be taught the language of instruction, especially the names for language parts including word, letter, and sentence; beginning and ending; and position words such as first, second, and third.

Take 2 Review

- Complete this two-column organizer.
- In the first column are restatements of main ideas. Work with the group or a partner to complete the second column. List a few details that elaborate the main ideas or that state the relevance of those ideas for your school or classroom.

Knowledge/Main Ideas	Application/Details
1. Phoneme awareness is a necessary, but not sufficient, step in learning to read and spell.	
2. It is important for teachers to know how to correctly pronounce English phonemes.	
3. When teaching phoneme awareness, it may be necessary to teach students to attend to larger linguistic units.	

Teaching Phoneme Awareness

For Whom Is Phoneme Awareness Instruction Important?

Students who benefit from direct teaching of phoneme awareness are those who are not able to orally segment and/or blend the single speech sounds in one-syllable words with accuracy and automaticity. This may include older students who did not master phoneme awareness when they were younger and who lack the foundation skills necessary for accurate decoding and spelling. Younger or older students who exhibit one or more of the following characteristics will benefit from instruction in phoneme awareness:

- They are typically below benchmark on DIBELS® (Dynamic Indicators of Basic Early Literacy Skills) (Good & Kaminski, 2003) phoneme segmentation fluency (PSF).
- They may not know the identity of the sounds in English (e.g., /sh/ and /ch/, or /b/ and /p/) and may be unable to replicate some sounds correctly.
- They cannot correctly segment phonemes in three- or four-sound spoken words.
- When reading, instead of blending all word sounds together, they usually guess at words on the basis of one or two of the sounds the letters represent.
- Their spelling may be incomplete, may include only one or two of the sounds in the word, or—in the case of very young learners—may be just a random string of letters.

Principles of Phoneme Awareness Instruction

The goal of phonological instruction is to enable students to remember, retrieve, and think about all the sounds in words—what researchers (Scarborough & Brady, 2002) call a *fully specified internal image* of a word. Students are most likely to succeed at beginning reading and spelling if they can automatically and accurately think about the sound structure of words, including syllables, onset and rime, and phonemes. When they can analyze spoken word parts, they can more readily connect sounds to print. Students who know letter-sound correspondences automatically are more likely to focus on meaning when they read.

Phonological instruction focuses on *spoken* language—not written—in the beginning stages, because many students need practice directing their attention to speech. Letters and print can be brought into lessons and matched to speech sounds as soon as students have demonstrated they are primed to focus on speech—that is, they are able to auditorily blend simple onset and rime (e.g., /s/ + /ăt/ = **sat**) and isolate initial sounds in words.

These basic principles of instruction in phoneme awareness are well validated by research (Gillon, 2004; NICHD, 2000; Scarborough & Brady, 2002):

1. Follow a progression of task difficulty, moving from the easiest tasks to the most difficult.
   - Identify and match the *initial* sounds in words, then final and middle sounds (e.g., "Find the pictures of things that begin with /m/"). Use simple words that the student knows.
   - Segment and produce an *initial* sound, then final and middle sounds (e.g., "What sound does **knee** start with?").
   - Begin with continuant sounds (e.g., /s/, /th/) and progress to stops (e.g., /p/, /t/).
   - Blend sounds into words (e.g., "Listen: /f/ /ē/ /t/. Say it fast.").
   - Segment the phonemes in two- or three-sound words (e.g., "The word is **eyes**. Stretch and say the sounds: /ī/ /z/"), moving to four and five sounds as the student becomes proficient.
   - Manipulate phonemes by deleting, adding, or substituting sounds (e.g., "Say **smoke** without the /m/"). (Use colored tiles or blocks to build a sound chain—**lamp, camp, cramp, crimp, crimps**.)
2. Focus student attention on *sound* before introducing letters. Practice phoneme awareness tasks until you are sure a student's "auditory antennae" are directed toward speech before introducing letter-sound associations.

> **Sample Activity:** Sort pictures into categories of words that begin with the same sound. Progress to sorting for the ending sound or middle sound.

3. Encourage *mouth awareness*. Phonemes are speech gestures as well as speech sounds. Articulation of the sounds is very important in developing awareness of them. Ask students whether their mouth is open or closed when they make the sound. Ask them if they are using their tongue, teeth, or lips when they make the sound.

> **Sample Activity:** Instruct students to look into a mirror when they say a letter sound or to watch you when you make letter sounds. Lead them to see how their teeth, tongue, and lips help to create sounds.

4. Introduce *all* sounds in your instruction, including vowel sounds (such as /ŏŏ/ in **foot**) and sounds typically spelled with more than one letter (such as /ch/ in **chin** and **itch**, or /t͟h/ in **that**).

> **Sample Activity:** Instead of an alphabetized word wall, create a "sound wall" that lists all of the speech sounds in English. Display consonant sounds on one wall and vowel sounds on another.

5. Use your hands, eyes, body, and mouth during instruction. Multisensory involvement keeps students' attention.

> **Sample Activity:** While saying three separate sounds in words such as **wave**, stand and touch head–waist–toes. This activity really gets students moving and segmenting!

6. Use guide words represented by gestures, pictures, and/or objects to help students identify and remember speech sounds.

> **Sample Activity:** Use pictures, gestures, and other associations to help students identify the more elusive sounds, such as short vowels (e.g., "/ĕ/ is the first sound in **edge**, so I can run my hand on the *edge* of the table while I make the sound").

7. A few brief (10–15 minutes) activities per day are all that most young students need to increase and improve awareness of speech.

Exercise 3.3 View a Video Demonstration of Phoneme Awareness Instruction

(*Teaching Reading Essentials* [Moats & Farrell, 2007], Part 2, Demonstration 6.)

- What are students being asked to do?

  ____

- Where is the task in the "ladder" of phonological skill development?

  ____

- What errors are students making?

  ____

- What kind of corrective feedback do students get?

  ____

- What multisensory techniques are being used?

  ____

(continued)

Exercise 3.3 (continued)

- Is the teacher using any guide words to help students identify sounds?

  ____

- Are the words appropriate for the task?

  ____

- What else would you do if you were the teacher?

  ____

- Where might the instruction go from here?

  ____

Chapter Review and Wrap-Up

- Work with a partner to write short answers to these questions:

  1. Why is phoneme awareness a critical skill for reading and spelling?

     ____

     ____

  2. Do I know where I can go to find word lists and activities for teaching phonological skills?

     ____

     ____

  3. What activities or skills am I likely to apply in my teaching?

     ____

     ____

What Else Is There to Learn About Phoneme Awareness?

LETRS *Module 2, The Speech Sounds of English: Phonetics, Phonology, and Phoneme Awareness* (Moats, 2004b), goes into greater depth on these topics:

- Coarticulation and why phonemes are elusive
- Schwa, diphthongs, and other details of phoneme identity and classification
- Differentiating units of speech from units of print
- Allophonic variation, or why phonemes are like chameleons when they are combined in spoken words
- How students' spelling reflects their phonological judgments and why spelling is a good diagnostic indicator of students' phoneme awareness
- Sequencing instructional activities from easy to progressively more difficult

Make a Connection to the Reading Program: Bridging Activities

Phonological Awareness: Bridging Activity

- Using the PA continuum, analyze the activities in your program. (Coaches and teachers should look at the kindergarten and first grade programs.)
- Do the activities follow a logical progression?
- Are the activities labeled correctly?
- What could you do to enhance instruction for struggling readers who lack PA?

Phonological Awareness: Bridging Activity

- Find the "Theme at a Glance" in your teacher's manual. Look under these two columns:
  - Phonemic Awareness
  - Phonics & Word Work
- What skills are introduced or reinforced?
- Are PA and Phonics distinguished?
- Is PA taught explicitly and systematically?

Phoneme Awareness: Bridging Activity

- Using the phoneme awareness progression, select words from your current anthology and create several activities.
- Teachers of older students will use vocabulary words to practice phoneme awareness as a warm-up before a word study lesson.

Chapter 4

Phonics

Learner Objectives for Chapter 4

- Explain the role of phonics in proficient reading.
- Review a brief history of reading instruction in the United States.
- Identify the characteristics of systematic, explicit phonics and contrast those with implicit, incidental approaches.
- Learn and define important terms in phonics instruction.
- Review a typical scope and sequence of phonics instruction.
- Identify the most and least regular phoneme-grapheme correspondences.
- Learn the technique of phoneme-grapheme mapping.
- Distinguish regular from irregular spellings.
- Role-play a few components of a typical phonics lesson.
- Critique a video demonstration of phonics instruction.

Warm-Up Questions

How confident are you about your answers to these questions? Circle the number that applies.

1 = not confident **2** = I know something **3** = pretty confident **4** = highly confident

1. What is the alphabetic principle?	1	2	3	4
2. Which phonics patterns should be taught?	1	2	3	4
3. Where is the research support for teaching phonics?	1	2	3	4
4. Is there a best way to teach phonics?	1	2	3	4
5. How can we identify who needs phonics instruction?	1	2	3	4
6. Is phonics instruction appropriate beyond the primary grades?	1	2	3	4

Good Readers Use Phonics!

A Definition of Phonics

Phonics is the *study of the relationships between letters and the sounds they represent*.The term is also used to describe code-emphasis or phonics approaches to reading instruction. Code-emphasis or phonics approaches organize beginning reading lessons around sound-symbol correspondences and teach students how to use sound-symbol associations while decoding and spelling new words.

One Essential Component

Phonics is one of the "five essential components" of reading instruction named in current federal and state policies governing the implementation of scientifically based reading research (SBRR). Among scientists who study reading, consensus is very strong that knowledge of phonics plays an important role in learning to read and spell, and that the most effective instruction teaches students to decode and spell new words by using sound-symbol correspondences (Ehri & Snowling, 2004; NICHD, 2000; Rayner et al., 2001). Knowledge of sound-symbol correspondences, in turn, facilitates learning to recognize words "by sight" or automatically. How did reading scientists arrive at that conclusion?

Figure 4.1 "Rope" Model of Reading Skill Development

The Many Strands that are Woven into Skilled Reading
(Scarborough, 2001)

LANGUAGE COMPREHENSION

BACKGROUND KNOWLEDGE
(facts, concepts, etc.)

VOCABULARY
(breadth, precision, links, etc.)

LANGUAGE STRUCTURES
(syntax, semantics, etc.)

VERBAL REASONING
(inference, metaphor, etc.)

LITERACY KNOWLEDGE
(print concepts, genres, etc.)

WORD RECOGNITION

PHONOLOGICAL AWARENESS
(syllables, phonemes, etc.)

DECODING (alphabetic principle, spelling-sound correspondences)

SIGHT RECOGNITION
(of familiar words)

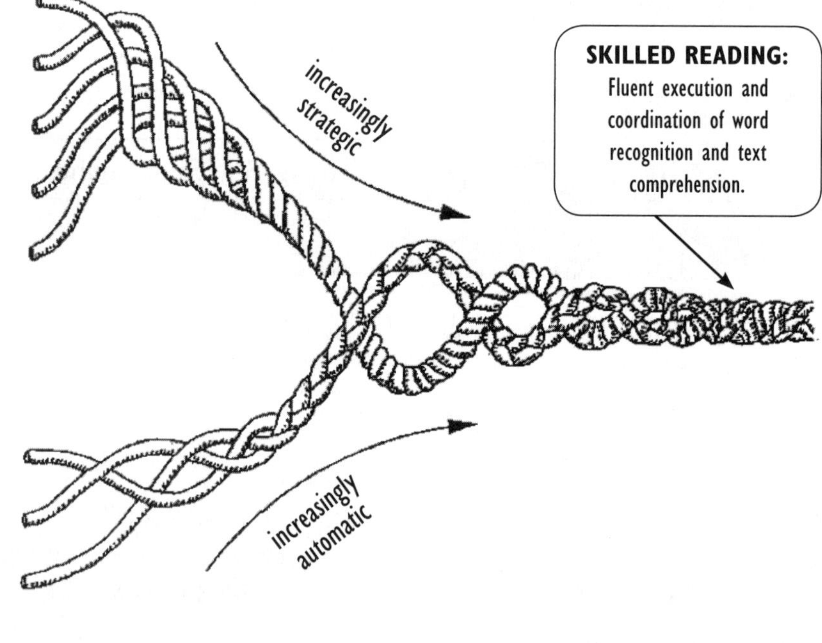
increasingly strategic
SKILLED READING:
Fluent execution and coordination of word recognition and text comprehension.
increasingly automatic

Used with permission of Hollis Scarborough.

The Alphabetic Principle

The English writing system uses an **alphabet**. English **orthography**, or writing, embodies the **alphabetic principle**. The alphabetic principle is the concept that letters and letter combinations (**graphemes**) represent the individual **phonemes** in words.

- map = /m/ /ă/ /p/
- shout = /sh/ /ou/ /t/
- read = /r/ /ē/ /d/ or /r/ /ĕ/ /d/ (depending on context)
- exact = /ĕ/ /g/ /z/ /ă/ /k/ /t/
- collar = /k/ /ŏ/ /l/ /er/

The alphabetic principle in the structure of the writing system allows us to read a word we have never seen before. Sometimes the alphabetic code allows us to only approximate the pronunciation of a word, as in **vicar**; we must then hear the word pronounced, have it defined, or see its use in context to fully identify it. The alphabetic principle is embodied in the phonics system of English. Other languages, such as Greek, Russian, and Hebrew, also employ the alphabetic principle in their written language systems.

The English alphabet is not perfectly designed for representing speech sounds. If it were, it would use only one letter for each phoneme in the language. As it is, English orthography often uses letter combinations for single phonemes (e.g., **th**, **aw**) instead of single letters, and it sometimes uses single letters (e.g., **e**, **y**, **c**) to represent several different sounds. Nevertheless, someone who knows the phonemes and graphemes (the spellings for phonemes) can approximate the identification of new words in English by blending the sounds, left to right.

The English alphabet is truly a miraculous invention—and a recent one! The English alphabet evolved first from the Phoenicians, then to the Greeks, and then to the Romans. The alphabetic writing system we use today was finally established in the 1800s when comprehensive dictionaries by Noah Webster and others were widely published.

How We Read New Words

In the diagram of the Four-Part Processor of the brain that supports word recognition (refer to Chapter 1, p. 24), phonics is the link between **orthography** and **phonology**. Phonics is a system of correspondences, patterns, and conventions by which speech is represented in print. The system of phoneme-grapheme correspondences can be learned and generalized to new words. In addition, the meanings of words (**semantics**) do influence how they are spelled (e.g., **they're**, **their**, **there**; **playground**; **unnatural**) and the origin, or **etymology**, of words also determines their spellings (e.g., **chlorophyll** is from Greek, so it uses **ch**, **ph**, and **y** for /k/, /f/, and /ĭ/ respectively). Therefore, printed word recognition is facilitated by knowledge of all of these language ingredients:

- *orthography* (letters, letter combinations, and their allowed sequences in the writing system)
- *phonology* (speech sound identification and recall)
- *semantics* (spellings for meaningful word parts and homophones)
- *etymology* (spellings retained from "donor" languages and other influences of language history)

Exercise 4.1 Read a New Word

noctambulist

- How did you do that? Very quickly, your mind:
  - recognized four syllables organized around vowels and the sounds in each syllable;
  - recognized meaningful parts that were familiar from other known words (*noct-* meaning "night," from Latin and German; *ambul-* meaning "to walk," from Latin *ambulare*; *ist*, an ending that marks the word as a noun);
  - connected a meaning with your background knowledge.
- In what context might you understand and possibly sympathize with the meaning of **noctambulist**?

  ____

- Now, read this sentence:

  The noctambulist has no memory of his midnight stroll to the kitchen, where he snacked on chocolate cake and ice cream.

- What does **noctambulist** mean?

  ____

Congratulations! You have just completed a very complex task of word recognition and comprehension by employing your knowledge of sound-symbol correspondences, knowledge of meaningful word parts, background knowledge, and ability to use language context to help decipher word meaning. Phonic knowledge, along with other language and cognitive skills, allowed you to decode an unknown word.

A Brief History of Phonics Instruction

Swings of the Pendulum

Reading instruction practices have undergone many changes over the past few hundred years. Since the Greeks and Plato, the "pendulum" of philosophies and methods for teaching people to read an alphabetic writing system has swung many times between *phonics-emphasis* approaches and *meaning-emphasis* approaches. Phonics-emphasis approaches teach students directly about the sounds that letters represent and emphasize the skill of sounding out new words by decoding their sounds. Meaning-emphasis approaches minimize direct teaching of the written orthographic code. Some go so far as to claim that phonics is destructive, evil, or an impediment to the enjoyment of reading.

Thus, phonics has not always been "in." In the pendulum swings of favored methods for teaching reading, phonics instruction at times has been relegated to dark closets and even expulsed from the classroom. For several periods during the 20th century, phonics was definitely "out," or at least was considered optional. There was little understanding of why phonics might be necessary or important. If students had difficulty learning and applying phonics to sound out unfamiliar words, "bypass strategies" such as memorization of whole words that involved no phonics were often recommended. A professor was once heard saying, "Some students wouldn't know a phonic if it kicked them in the shin!"

The Evolution of Research-Based Reading Instruction

Noah Webster initiated the first era of phonics-based reading instruction in the United States with his *Blue-Backed Speller* in 1806. This popular speller was used by millions of Americans to teach their children how to read and helped to standardize English spelling. (Benjamin Franklin used Webster's speller to teach his granddaughter how to read.) Immigrants who did not speak English used Webster's speller as a tool to learn to speak, read, and spell the language. By 1861, 1 million copies were sold per year. This book helped to launch the practice of the spelling bee.

Then, in the mid-1800s, a second era in reading instruction began when Horace Mann, the secretary of education in Massachusetts, wrote this about phonics: "It is upon this emptiness, blankness, silence and death, that we compel children to fasten their eyes; the odor and fungeousness of spelling book paper; a soporific effluvium seems to emanate from the page, steeping all their faculties in lethargy" (quoted by Balmuth, 1992, p. 190). Mann's strong sentiment regarding phonics had sweeping consequences for reading instruction. Mann's wife, Mary Peabody Mann, wrote the first "look-and-say" reader based on the ideas of Thomas Gallaudet, who developed reading material for the deaf, in which an opening sentence reads, "Frank had a dog; his name was Spot." Spot was in for a long and popular life!

Scott Foresman published look-and-say readers beginning in 1914. Spot the dog reappeared in the "Dick and Jane" reading series in the 1930s. Look-and-say reading instruction was dominant in reading instruction, even though parents were being told more and more often that their children needed remedial help. In the 1950s, illiteracy rates were increasing. The stage was thus set for Rudolph Flesch (1955) to publish his provocative book, *Why Johnny Can't Read*, in an attempt to resurface phonics as an important component of learning to read. Said Flesch (1955): "The truth is, of course, that any normal six-year-old loves to learn letters and sounds. He is fascinated by them. They are the greatest thing he has come up against in life." Research reviews, government-funded studies, and essays by Jeanne Chall (1967) helped to bring phonics back into favor for about 10–15 years until the next era of reading instruction took hold.

A Historical Summary of Reading Instruction in the United States

- **Early 1800s**—Children were taught to read by memorizing the alphabet, learning spelling correspondences, writing spelling lists, and reading the Bible and other "character-building" stories. Webster's *Blue-Backed Speller* was published in 1806.

- **Mid-1800s**—Horace Mann and others denounce phonics as vile and wicked, urging a change to meaning-based instruction.

- **1914**—Scott Foresman publishes the first look-and-say primers, organized by grade level.

- **1930–1965**—"Dick and Jane" readers—a look-and-say series emphasizing high-frequency words and sight word memorization—predominate. Phonics was an optional "add-on" in some schools.

- **1955**—Rudolph Flesch publishes *Why Johnny Can't Read*, an emotional diatribe against whole-word approaches that is intended to revive phonics instruction.

- **1967**—Jeanne Chall publishes *Learning to Read: The Great Debate*, a scholarly review of reading research that supports phonics instruction within a comprehensive program.

- **1960s–early 1970s**—Ayres (1972), Frostig (1965), and Kephart (1960), among others, promote the idea that students who struggled with reading were deficient in visual and perceptual motor skills and required extensive practice crawling, walking balance beams, and visually discriminating between geometric shapes that were the same and different.

- **1970s**—Whole-language philosophy evolves in Australia, New Zealand, and North America, urging a return to meaning-based instruction with "authentic" children's literature and warning that phonics instruction is unnecessary and an impediment to good reading.

- **1974**—Isabel Liberman, Alvin Liberman, and Donald Shankweiler at the Haskins Laboratories at Yale publish their first studies showing the strong relationship between phoneme awareness, word recognition, and spelling, pointing educators toward a critical link between language and literacy

- **1984**—*Becoming a Nation of Readers* (Anderson, Hiebert, Scott, & Wilkinson, 1985), published by the National Academy of Education, urges attention to reading research and supports the efficacy of phonics in a comprehensive English program.

- **1990**—Marilyn Adams (1990), commissioned to review reading research by the U.S. Department of Education, publishes *Beginning to Read*. This award-winning work of scholarship explains, on the basis of cognitive and linguistic studies, why phoneme awareness and phonics, along with comprehension, are essential components of language instruction. The national debate ("the Reading Wars") heats up.

- **1996**—California, after embracing whole-language standards and practices in 1987, reverses itself in the face of reading achievement declines and adopts regulations supporting explicit phonics- and research-based language instruction.
- **1998**—The federal Reading Excellence Act provides funds for research-based programs.
- **2000**—The National Reading Panel (NICHD, 2000), convened by Congress, publishes results of meta-analyses of rigorous research supporting "five essential components" of reading instruction; this report spawns funding for the Reading First initiative.
- **Present**—"Balanced literacy" continues as a popular alternative to systematic, explicit, phonics-emphasis approaches; all publishers claim their products are research-based, diminishing the importance of that term. Most approaches include some phonics instruction, although the quality and effectiveness vary widely. Phonics is "in," but practices range from incidental, unsystematic teaching to very structured, explicit, systematic teaching.

In the early 1970s, a third era of reading instruction was ushered in with the advent of a "new" reading philosophy vigorously advocated by its proponents. This approach, called **whole language**, championed *authentic* readers, children's literature, and learning to read from context and exposure. Phonics was not only out of favor, it was also demonized as a barrier against learning to read, even though all objective research summaries up until that time supported the value of phonics instruction. Instead of the familiar vocabulary of Dick and Jane, students were given books with many sophisticated and novel words meant to replicate "natural" language patterns, words whose pronunciations and meanings students were to guess from the context of the passage being read. Teachers were warned against "taking words apart" or being analytical about the skills necessary to support reading acquisition.

Whole language was a disaster for children who had not already learned to use the alphabetic code when they entered school. National test results in the 1990s, showing declines in reading achievement in states such as California that had embraced whole language, precipitated action on the part of lawmakers. When more than 40 percent of the nation's fourth graders were unable to demonstrate satisfactory reading skills on the National Assessment of Educational Progress, state and federal officials undertook a serious reassessment of standards, methods, and textbooks for reading instruction. Subsequently, Congress mandated a federally sponsored synthesis of reading research that eventually was published as the "Report of the National Reading Panel" (NICHD, 2000).

Where Are We Now?

What are colleges of education teaching new teachers about phonics and other aspects of reading instruction? The National Council on Teacher Quality recently completed a study to answer this question (Walsh, Glaser, & Dunne-Wilcox, 2006). Syllabi and textbooks from more than 250 reading-instruction courses were analyzed to determine if and how systematic and explicit phonics instruction, along with all essential components of instruction, was addressed in typical reading instruction courses. The findings demonstrated that many course syllabi and textbooks pay some attention to phonics, but the information remains simplistic and confusing, characterized by surface treatment, brief explanations, and inaccurately defined terms. It appears from this study and others that meaningful exposure to explicit and systematic phonics is somewhat difficult to come by. Some textbooks continue to dismiss explicit phonics as undesirable while promoting implicit, teach-as-you-need-it phonics. No wonder teachers are often confused about the best way to go.

Textbook publishers are changing their programs, however, to comply with Reading First guidelines and state standards for both teachers and students. Most of the publishers of core, comprehensive programs have fairly strong phonics components in their new offerings, and there are many strong phonics intervention programs on the market. The Florida Center for Reading Research (www.fcrr.org) publishes unbiased reviews to help consumers find good teaching tools. The What Works Clearinghouse (www.whatworks.ed.gov/), directed by the U.S. Department of Education, also provides reviews of reading programs.

Contrasting Approaches

Some currently popular approaches to reading instruction continue to emphasize comprehension instruction over phonics and language skills and claim to be supported by reading research. Many of these go under the name of "whole language" or "balanced literacy" approaches. When the wrapping is removed from many "balanced literacy" programs, however, one does not usually find a *systematic, explicit, complete* phonics component or even a *systematic, explicit* vocabulary and comprehension component. That's what can be difficult to distinguish, especially for a person new to reading instruction.

In a systematic, explicit, phonics-emphasis program, the teacher organizes his or her instruction according to a preplanned sequence of phonics and word-recognition skills, from easier to more difficult. Vocabulary and comprehension are also taught, but the primary emphasis in the beginning stages is on getting students to read the print without relying on pictures or memorization. A basic assumption is that if students learn the phonics code and acquire independent word-recognition skills, they will be able to read words accurately and will then be more likely to read fluently for comprehension. Phoneme/grapheme correspondences are taught cumulatively and thoroughly in the first stages of instruction, with increasing emphasis on text reading as students become proficient in reading the words. In the first few months of instruction, comprehension and vocabulary are developed through reading aloud and oral-language comprehension until students can read text for meaning. In a systematic phonics approach, students are taught to: (1) look carefully at the word; (2) sound the word out; and (3) check to see

Contrasting Approaches

Systematic, Explicit	Incidental, Embedded
• Preplanned scope and sequence	• Opportunistic, as children make errors
• Easy to more difficult	• No predetermined sequence
• Cumulative review	• Skills taught in mini-lessons, as needed
• "I do, We do, You do"	• Insufficient practice for students at risk
• Guided practice to independent practice	

if the pronounced word makes sense in the passage. Decodable text, with many examples of the phonics patterns already taught, is used to provide practice as new skills are introduced.

Contrasting Strategies

Systematic, Explicit	Incidental, Embedded
• Look carefully at the word. • Sound it out. • Check it (use the context to resolve meaning).	• Think about what would make sense here. • Read the whole sentence. • Look at the pictures. • Look at the first letter. • Sound it out (last resort).

Whole language and balanced literacy approaches, in contrast, promote context-based strategies for teaching word recognition. The important component of instruction, phonics, represents a primary difference between methods. In whole-language approaches, students are encouraged to guess unknown words from pictures, context, and a few letters, or to memorize whole words and repetitious language patterns in the text ("predictable text"). Phonics may receive some attention, but the instruction may be haphazard, implicit, and lacking in the kind of extended practice that many students need. The phonics instruction may not be connected to the books that students are asked to read. Most importantly, nonsystematic approaches may be ineffective for "average" to "low average" students who need phonics, phoneme awareness, and fluency-building along with vocabulary and comprehension instruction in order to progress at an optimal rate.

Who Needs Phonics, and How Do We Know?

Cumulative scientific research gathered over the past several decades provides evidence that the alphabetic principle and explicit, systematic phonics are important components of reading instruction for all students (Ehri, 2004). Dozens of studies were summarized in the Report of the National Reading Panel (NICHD, 2000), and evidence continues to support the report's conclusion. Systematic phonics instruction is generally associated with improved ability to read words, spell accurately, comprehend text, and read text orally with sufficient speed to support understanding. Phonics, built on a foundation of phoneme awareness and letter knowledge, is most important for students who struggle with learning to read, including minority students, ELL students, and those in the lower half of the distribution of reading skill.

Phonics instruction should begin as soon as children can identify two and three phonemes in spoken words and when they know their alphabet letters. Typically, this is during the last half of kindergarten. A series of studies on the prediction of later reading outcomes has shown how important this step can be in building later reading fluency and comprehension (Good, Simmons, & Kame'enui, 2001; Torgesen, 2005). It should continue until students know all the major phoneme/grapheme correspondences and syllable patterns and can make a good attempt to decode any unfamiliar word (Ehri & Snowling, 2004).

Students are likely to benefit from phonics instruction if they:

- are stymied or guess wildly when they approach unfamiliar words
- cannot associate phonemes and graphemes with accuracy and fluency
- have trouble blending sounds into words
- spell poorly
- score low on a test of reading nonsense syllables
- score low on a test of reading real words out of context

Advanced phonics instruction moves beyond phoneme/grapheme correspondences. This component should continue through at least second and third grade. Instruction emphasizes how to break down and decode words of more than one syllable. The sounds of vowel spellings are related to the six basic syllable types in English. In addition, the meaningful parts of words (i.e., morphemes) and word history are taught systematically. If older students are not accurate and fluent in word recognition, they will still need a strong phonics and word study component in their reading programs.

Where Else Is the Evidence to Support the Value of Phonics?

Additional support for phonics instruction can be found in eye-movement research in cognitive psychology, studies of the reading brain at work, and studies of instruction since the publication of the Report of the National Reading Panel (NICHD, 2000).

- Eye-movement studies help us understand that proficient readers perceive and register all the letters in words while reading (Rayner et al., 2001).
- Results from a complex series of recent studies known as the Early Interventions Project documented the importance of students learning the alphabetic principle and mastering the step of phoneme awareness (Foorman & Moats, 2004). At-risk children scored above average in word recognition, phonic decoding, and spelling at the end of first grade—and tended to be better at all reading skills, including passage comprehension at the end of second grade—when phonics instruction was strong (Foorman & Schatschneider, 2003).
- When a whole-language tutorial approach is modified with a systematic, explicit phonics component added to instructional routines, students progress significantly faster and more students reach grade level (Chapman, Tunmer, & Prochnow, 2001).
- Studies since 2000 continue to show an advantage for programs that include systematic, explicit instruction in the orthographic code of English, such as the study abstracted here.

Abstract of Research Study on Decoding Skills*

This study compared the efficacy of two decoding skill–based programs, one based on explicit orthographic rime and one on grapheme/phoneme correspondences, to a control group exposed to an implicit phonics program. Children in both explicit decoding programs performed consistently better than the control group in the accuracy with which they read and spelled words covered in the program. Only children in the grapheme/phoneme correspondence group consistently read words more quickly than children in the control group. Children in both explicit decoding programs scored higher than the children in the control group on measures of reading comprehension and oral reading at posttest.

* Christenson, C. A., & Bowey, J. A. (2005). The efficacy of orthographic rime, grapheme-phoneme correspondence, and implicit phonics approaches to teaching decoding skills. *Scientific Studies of Reading, 9*(4), 327–349.

Phonics Defined: Know Your Terminology!

This section will briefly teach the most common phonics terms, provide examples of those terms in words, and then, through interactive exercises, practice and review the information.

Exercise 4.2 Explore the Meanings of Phonics Terms

- Cut out the 12 letter (grapheme) tiles or copy them onto sticky notes. Use them to explore the phonics terms as they are presented.
- Note that each two-letter combination—**th**, **ck**, and **ng**—represents one speech sound. In addition, the three-letter combinations—**dge** and **igh**—represent one speech sound. Each grapheme tile represents a single speech sound for this exercise.

-dge	b	r	th	y	igh	i	ck	ng	t	l	s

(Some words that can be made from these graphemes are **bridge**, **bridges**, **light**, **lightly**, **thing**, **things**, **brick**, **thick**, **stick**, **sticky**, and **thigh**.)

Grapheme: A letter or group of letters used to spell a phoneme.
Task: Point to a grapheme tile with more than one letter. Say the sound represented by the grapheme.

Consonant. A speech sound that is created by a partial or complete obstruction of the air stream by any of various constrictions of the lips, tongue, teeth, throat, etc., such as /p/, /f/, /r/, /w/, and /h/. Consonant graphemes represent consonant phonemes.
Task: Group the consonant graphemes, and put the vowels (i.e., **igh**, **i**, **y**) aside. Say the sound represented by each consonant grapheme. Select one consonant grapheme. What part of the mouth is used to constrict or close off the air stream when you say the sound?

Consonant digraph. Two consonant letters that represent one sound; that sound is not represented by either letter singly. For example, the grapheme **sh** is a digraph. It does not represent /s/ or /h/. It spells its own sound, /sh/.
Task: Find a consonant digraph. What sound does it represent? Say a word that uses this grapheme.

Consonant blend: Two or three separate consonant sounds that occur as a cluster before or after the vowel in a syllable, such as **gl-**, **scr-**, and **-ft**. Consonant blends have separate sounds: **gl-**, while blended, still has two distinct separate phonemes: /g/ and /l/.
Task: Make a consonant blend with two of your tiles. Say the sounds separately. Blend the sounds together, and put them in a real word.

Exercise 4.2 (continued)

Vowel: Vowel graphemes represent vowel phonemes. Vowels are open sounds. Every syllable has one vowel sound. The most familiar vowel graphemes are **a**, **e**, **i**, **o**, and **u**, but vowel graphemes often use letter teams to represent vowel sounds, such as **igh**, **oy**, **ue**, and **oa**.
Task: Group the vowel graphemes (i.e., **igh**, **i**, **y**). What grapheme can represent either a consonant or a vowel phoneme?

Syllable: A unit of spoken language organized around a single vowel sound that may or may not have consonants before or after the vowel.
Task: Spell a one-syllable word with your tiles. Spell a two-syllable word. What vowel graphemes (i.e., **igh**, **i**, **y**) are in your syllables?

Orthography: A writing system. When we study a language's orthography, we study its spelling, spacing conventions, and capitalization and punctuation marks.
Task: Spell the word your trainer dictates to you. Discuss the orthography of this word with your partner. How many graphemes in the word? How many letters? Is there an unusual spelling for this word? Are there alternate spellings for this word? What else can you say about the word **orthography**?

Content of Phonics Instruction: What Should Be Taught?

Consonant Phoneme-Grapheme Correspondences

Common spellings (graphemes) are listed in the following chart for each of the consonant sounds. Note that the term *grapheme* refers to a letter or letter combination that corresponds to one speech sound.

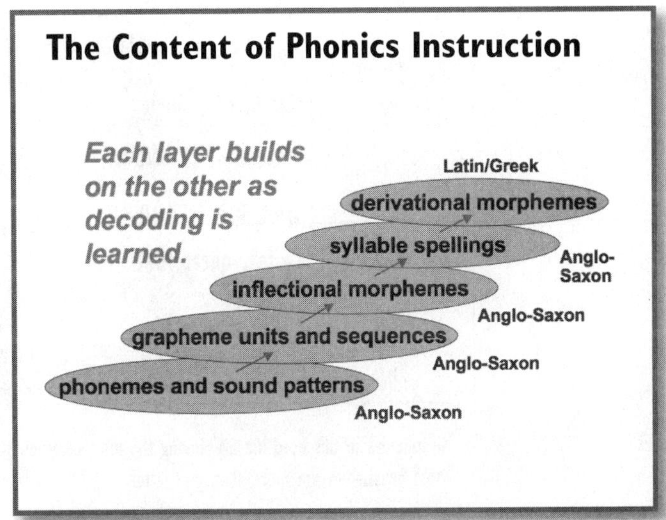

Consonant Phoneme-Grapheme Correspondence Chart		
Phoneme	**Word Examples**	**Graphemes for Spelling***
/p/	pit, spider, stop	p
/b/	bit, brat, bubble	b
/m/	mitt, comb, hymn	m, mb, mn
/t/	tickle, mitt, sipped	t, tt, ed
/d/	die, loved	d, ed
/n/	nice, knight, gnat	n, kn, gn
/k/	cup, kite, duck, chorus, folk, quiet	k, c, ck, ch, lk, q
/g/	girl, Pittsburgh	g, gh
/ng/	sing, bank	ng, n
/f/	fluff, sphere, tough, calf	f, ff, gh, ph, lf
/v/	van, dove	v, ve
/s/	sit, pass, science, psychic	s, ss, sc, ps
/z/	zoo, jazz, nose, as, Xerox	z, zz, se, s, x
/th/	thin, breath, ether	th
/<u>th</u>/	this, breathe, either	th
/sh/	shoe, mission, sure, charade, precious, notion, mission, special	sh, ss, s, ch, sc, ti, si, ci
/zh/	measure, azure	s, z
/ch/	cheap, future, etch	ch, tch
/j/	judge, wage	j, dge, ge
/l/	lamb, call, single	l, ll, le
/r/	reach, wrap, her, fur, stir	r, wr, er/ur/ir
/y/	you, use, feud, onion	y, (u, eu), i
/w/	witch, queen, one	w, (q)u, (w)o
/wh/	where	wh
/h/	house, whole	h

* Graphemes in this word list are among the most common spellings, but the list does not include all possible graphemes for a given consonant. Most graphemes are more than one letter.

Vowel Phoneme-Grapheme Correspondences

Common spellings (graphemes) are presented within words in the following chart for the vowel sounds explored in Chapter 3.

Vowel Phoneme-Grapheme Correspondence Chart		
Phoneme	**Word Examples**	**Graphemes for Spelling***
/ē/	see, these, me, eat, key, happy, chief, either	ee, e_e, -e, ea, ey, -y, ie, ei
/ĭ/	sit, gym	i, y
/ā/	make, rain, play, great, baby, eight, vein, they	a_e, ai, ay, ea, -y, eigh, ei, ey
/ĕ/	bed, breath	e, ea
/ă/	cat	a
/ī/	time, pie, cry, right, rifle	i_e, ie, -y, igh, -i
/ŏ/	fox, swap, palm	o, wa, al
/ŭ/	cup, cover, flood, tough	u, o, oo, ou
/aw/	saw, pause, call, water, bought	aw, au, all, wa, ough
/ō/	vote, boat, toe, snow, open	o_e, oa, oe, ow, o-,
/o͝o/	took, put, could	oo, u, ou
/ū/ (/o͞o/)	moo, tube, blue, chew, suit, soup	oo, u_e, ue, ew, ui, ou
/y/ /ū/	use, few, cute	u, ew, u_e
/oi/	boil, boy	oi, oy
/ow/	out, cow	ou, ow
/er/	her, fur, sir	er, ur, ir
/ar/	cart	ar
/or/	sport	or
schwa	<u>a</u>bout, less<u>o</u>n, <u>e</u>lect, def<u>i</u>nition, circ<u>u</u>s	a, o, e, i, u

* The word examples in the list present the most common spellings, but the list does not include all possible graphemes for a given vowel. Most graphemes are more than one letter.

- Short vowel sounds are almost always spelled with single vowel letters, as follows:

Sound-spelling cards from *Spelling by Pattern, Level I* (Javernick and Moats, 2007).

- Long vowel sounds are more complicated because there are more ways to spell them, and the correspondences are not as predictable. Diphthongs—the "sliding" vowels—are different because we shift the position of our mouth to say them.

Exercise 4.3 Hunt for the Code

- Use the Phoneme-Grapheme Correspondence Charts to answer these questions:
  1. Which consonant sounds have the least consistent spellings? The most consistent?

     ____

  2. Which vowel sounds have the least consistent spellings? The most consistent?

     ____

  3. Which spellings have your students learned, and which are taught at the grade level you teach?

     ____

     ____

Teaching Phoneme-Grapheme Correspondences and Word Recognition

Reflection

If you were learning to play a musical instrument to improve your musical ability, what would enable you to learn best: exposure to lots of good music or direct, sequential, cumulative, and systematic instruction, with lots of practice? Or both? If we are learning a new task, we undoubtedly expect our instruction (especially if we are paying for it!) to be carefully planned and presented in a way that will help us learn it well and become confident in our skills! In what other ways is learning to read like learning to master any other skill?

What Is Explicit and Systematic Phonics?

Explicit and *systematic* are common terms frequently used when phonics is being discussed. These terms deserve more specific explanation, because many instructional texts and reading programs are not clear about what "explicit" teaching is and what "systematic" means.

- **Explicit.** The information to be learned is **ex**plained and taught to students. The concept is put out, made transparent, as in **ex-**, which means "out." The skill is clearly presented, discussed, explained, and taught, leaving nothing to guesswork. Explicit instruction demystifies the phonics system. Explicit instruction provides a lot more direction and support for students than incidental teaching or teaching that simply corrects errors.
- **Systematic *skills sequence*.** When phonics is taught systematically, *a predetermined sequence of skills guides the order in which phonic elements are introduced.* Those skills are then practiced through reading material, with multiple examples of words with the

phonic element just learned. Systematic instruction alleviates the hit-or-miss game that is common when teachers constantly create their own lessons.

- **Systematic *lesson format*.** Systematic can also refer to a predictable lesson format with instructional routines. A systematic lesson unfolds in this order:
  1. The teacher explicitly teaches a skill ("I Do").
  2. Students are guided and supported as they practice the skill ("We Do").
  3. Students practice the skill independently with teacher monitoring ("You Do").

What Are the Typical Routines of Systematic, Explicit Phonics Instruction?

A lesson is usually structured around routines that: (a) provide review; (b) introduce a new concept; and (c) offer various kinds of practice. A general framework designed to provide students with enough practice to apply phonics skills to reading and writing is as follows:

- State the lesson objective and purpose.
- Review.
- Identify sounds in words (sound warm-up).
- Match letters to sounds and vice versa.
- Teach the new letter-sound correspondence pattern.
- Blend sounds together into words.
- Teach "heart words" (irregular words).
- Practice to build fluency:
  - Conduct question-and-answer games (e.g., "Read the word that means . . . ")
  - Conduct timed speed drills.
  - Demonstrate pattern recognition (e.g., underline the rime in several words, then ask students to read the rime and then the whole word).
  - Conduct word-sorting exercises.
- Read words in context (connected text reading such as phrases and sentences).
- Read decodable text to practice recognizing words with known patterns.
- Spell words, write sentences.

Exercise 4.4 Role-Play and Discuss "soft **c**" Lesson

- Role-play a systematic and explicit lesson that teaches the letter **c** spells the /s/ sound.
- Follow your presenter's instructions to see what a systematic and explicit lesson feels like, or role-play with a partner.

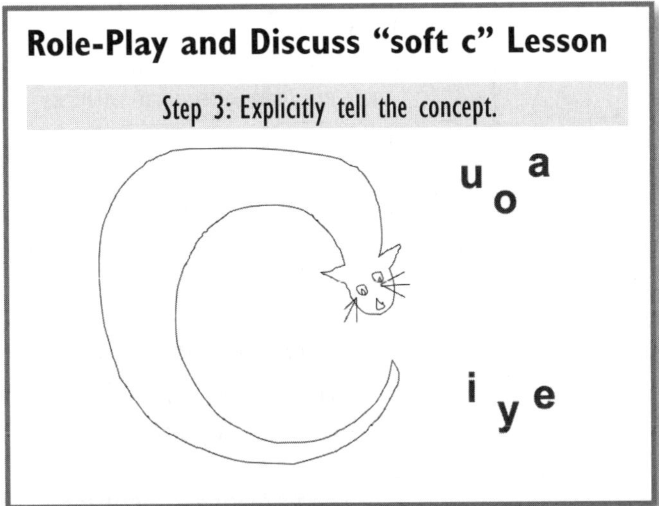
Role-Play and Discuss "soft c" Lesson
Step 3: Explicitly tell the concept.
u o a
i y e

Lesson Structure	Lesson Content
1. State purpose for lesson.	Teacher: "Today we will read and spell some words that use the letter **c** for the sound /s/. Sometimes **c** stands for /k/, and sometimes it stands for /s/."
2. Isolate phoneme awareness.	Teacher: "Listen while I say some words. [Teacher models the following gestures.] If you hear /k/ at the beginning, say /k/ and make your scraping motion, /k/ /k/ /k/. If you hear /s/ at the beginning, say /s/ and make your snake motion." **cent city cyclone carry cot circus**
3. Explicitly tell the concept.	Teacher: Display a picture of Momma **C** Cat with her babies **i**, **e**, **y**, and **a**, **o**, **u**. Say: "Momma **C** Cat's babies **a**, **o**, **u** are such good little children, they make her purr, /kkkkk/. But **e**, **i**, **y** are naughty children and make her hiss, /sssssss/. The letter **c** can stand for /s/ when it is followed by **e**, **i**, or **y**, as in **cent**, **city**, or **cyclone**. We call it *soft* or *hissing* **c**." *

(continued)

Exercise 4.4 (continued)

Lesson Structure	Lesson Content
4. Check student memory.	Teacher: "When can the letter **c** stand for the sound /s/?" Students: "When it is followed by [**e**, **i**, or **y**]."
Have some fun!	Teacher: "Here's a song that can help us remember (sing to "Old MacDonald Had a Farm")": ** There are three letters that soften **c**, E I E I Y. Teacher: Show Momma **C** Cat. Hold up individual vowel letter cards (**a**, **e**, **i**, **o**, **u**) to her right. Ask: "What does Momma **C** Cat say?"
5. "**I Do**" (teacher demonstration)	Teacher: "Let's blend some words with the soft **c** sound, /s/. First, I'll say the sounds as I point to them. Then, I'll say the whole word as I move my finger underneath." **cent rice cinder icy**
6. "**We Do**" (teacher and students together)	Teacher: "Now, you 'touch and say' with these words. You say the sounds as I point to them, and blend the word as I trace underneath it with my finger." **acid face cell recipe nice cymbal** (Multisyllabic words can be read one syllable at a time, then blended.)
7. "**You Do**" (students practice independently)	Teacher: "Now, get ready to read these words with soft **c** (/s/). First, underline **c** and the vowel that follows it on your paper. [*pause*] Now, touch and say each word." **citrus peace spicy fence**
8. Read the words in sentences.	It is a <u>cinch</u> to write with this <u>nice</u> <u>pencil</u>. <u>Nancy</u> fell off her <u>bicycle</u> <u>twice</u> on the <u>icy</u> path.

Exercise 4.4 (continued)

Lesson Structure	Lesson Content
9. Read a simple decodable story. ***	(Systematic programs provide stories and informational text for extended practice in reading words with phonic elements that have been taught.)
10. Spell some words, and write sentences to dictation.	Teacher dictates a few words and a sentence to provide additional practice and to build automaticity with the skill.

* The Momma Cat story was shared with us by a phonics teacher who can no longer identify where she learned it. We, and everyone who learns it, love to use it to teach the soft and hard sounds of **c**.

** The "soft **c**" song, to the tune of "Old MacDonald Had a Farm," is credited to Kathi Grace (2007), author of *Phonics and Spelling Through Phoneme-Grapheme Mapping.*

*** "The Race" (by Deborah Glaser): Cindy helped me move the dirt by the fence to fill a hole. It was a race to see who could place the dirt in the center of the hole first. When we were done, not a trace was left in the space, and the nice man gave us a fancy cent to go to the circus.

A Sample Skills Sequence for the Primary Grades

The phonics concept that **c** = /s/ when followed by **e**, **i**, or **y** is advanced and is taught to students after they have already learned many other phonics concepts. The following chart is a possible sequence of skills showing at what point the concept of "soft **c**" might be explicitly taught. (Start reading down the first column, then continue into the second column.) Study this sequence of skills, and then answer these questions:

1. What skills have students learned prior to learning the "soft **c**" concept that prepared them to be able to read the sample words in Exercise 4.4?

____

____

____

2. A skills sequence is an integral part of systematic phonics lessons. What are the advantages of having a skills sequence for the teacher? For students?

____

____

____

Sample Skills Sequence (Primary Grades)*

1. First consonants and vowels: c o a d g m l h t	22. th (unvoiced, as in **think**)	40. er (as in **term**)
2. i (as in **itch**)	23. qu (as in **quilt**)	41. ir (as in **sir**)
3. j	24. Two-syllable compound words	42. ur (as in **hurt**)
4. k	25. Spelling rule: double ff-ll-ss	43. ow (as in **cow**)
5. p	26. Two closed syllables	44. ou (as in **out**)
6. ch (as in **chip**)	27. Consonant blends	45. igh (as in **night**)
7. u (as in **up**)	28. Two closed syllables with consonant blends	46. Consonant-**le** syllables: -ble -fle -tle -dle -gle -kle -ple -zle
8. b	29. Nasal rime patterns: -ing -ang -ong -ung -ink -ank -onk -unk	47. Odd long-vowel words: -ild -old -ind -ost -olt
9. r	30. "magic **e**"or CV-**e**	48. ar (as in **art**)
10. f	31. Two-syllable words containing "magic **e**"	49. or (as in **born**)
11. n	32. ph (as in **phrase**)	50. oo (as in **moon**)
12. e (as in **echo**)	33. ea (as in **meat**)	51. Endings: **-ly** and **y**
13. s (as in **sun**)	34. oa (as in **boat**)	52. ck (as in **back**)
14. sh	35. ai (as in **pain**)	53. Hard-soft **c**
15. th (voiced, as in **this**)	36. ee (as in **bee**)	54. Hard-soft **g**
16. w	37. ay (as in **day**)	55. ge -dge
17. wh	38. oe (as in **doe**)	56. etc.
18. y (as in **yellow**)	39. Syllable division	
19. v		
20. x		
21. z		

* This sequence was adapted with permission from Educators Publishing Service: *Recipe for Reading Sequence Chart* (Traub & Bloom, 2004).

A Sample Skills Sequence for Older Students

This sequence is designed for older (middle and high school) students who do not know their vowels, have trouble reading multisyllabic words, and need help with the foundation of phoneme awareness.

Phonics Blitz* Scope and Sequence

Lesson	One-Minute Timed Oral Reading	Phonemic Awareness	Phonics
1	Each lesson begins with one-minute timed readings.	None	Introduce oral reading. Teach letter sounds: short vowels, consonants, digraphs.
2	One student is the Warm-Up Reader who reads aloud to the class for one minute, and the whole class marks any reading errors made.	*Explain that vowels can be sounds or letters* (e.g., long/short **a**).	Introduce closed syllables. Introduce "build a word" and "touch and say."
3		*Review* long/short **a**.	Read nonsense words and explain why they are important. Introduce word sorts and word lists.
4		long/short **i**	Introduce sentences. Digraph **-ck** occurs at the end of a 1-1-1 word.
5	After the Warm-Up Reader finishes, all students read aloud in pairs for one minute.	*Cumulative review*	Trigraphs
6		long/short **o**	Two-sound blends
7		*Cumulative review*	Three-sound blends
8		Identifying syllables	-ing, -ang, -ong, -ung, -ink, -ank, -onk, -unk
9	All students chart their accuracy percentage and WCPM at the beginning of each lesson. The goal is to reach at least 98% accuracy regularly, then to improve WCPM.	*Review syllables*	Reading multisyllabic words: two syllables
10		long/short **e**	Schwa
11		*Cumulative review*	Reading multisyllabic words: three or more syllables
12		long/short **u** /yu/	Spelling multisyllabic words
13		*Cumulative review*	Three sounds of suffix -ed
14		/o͞o/ (**school**)	Pay attention to suffixes. Vowel vs. consonant suffixes.
15		/oi/ + diphthong	1-1-1 doubling rule for one-syllable words

(continued)

Phonics Blitz **Scope and Sequence***			
Lesson	**One-Minute Timed Oral Reading**	**Phonemic Awareness**	**Phonics**
16	Oral reading at the beginning of each lesson lets the teacher and students know if *Phonics Blitz* instruction is transferring to non-decodable reading at a selected grade level.	/ou/ + diphthong	Hard **c** / soft **c**. **Y** as a vowel spells three sounds: short **i** (**gym**), long **i** (**hi**), long **e** (**happy**).
17		/ŏŏ/ (**cook**)	Hard **g** / soft **g**
18		/or/	Consonant **-le**
19		/ar/	Other spellings of /əl/: -el (**channel**), -il (**tonsil**), -al (**rascal**)
20		/er/	**r**-controlled vowels: /or/ and /ar/
21		*Add comprehension questions to oral reading passages in place of phonemic awareness.*	Spellings of /er/: -er, -ir, -ur, -ear
22			Spellings of /er/: -or, -ar
23			Open syllables
24			Vowel Consonant **e**: single-syllable words
25			Vowel Consonant **e**: multisyllabic words
26			Vowel Consonant **e**: schwa in VC**e** syllables at the end of words
27			Drop **e** when adding vowel suffixes
28			Spellings of long **o**: o, oa, ow, oe, o_e, -ough
29			Spellings of long **a**: a, ai, ay, a_e, -eigh, ea
30			Spellings of long **i**: i, ie, y, -igh, i_e
31			Spellings of long **e**: e, ee, ea, ie, y, ye, e_e
32			Spellings of long **u** /yu/: u, u_e, ue, ew
33			Spellings of /ōō/ (**school**): u, oo, ou, ew, u_e, ue

Phonics Blitz Scope and Sequence*			
Lesson	**One-Minute Timed Oral Reading**	**Phonemic Awareness**	**Phonics**
34			Spellings of /oi/: oi, oy
35			Spellings of /ŏŏ/ (**book**): oo, u
36			Spellings of /ou/: ow, ou
37			Spellings of /aw/: aw, au
38			OW spells two sounds: /ō/, /ou/
39			OO spells two sounds: /ōō/ (**school**), /ŏŏ/ (**book**)
40			Two vowels together, each in a different syllable

* This scope and sequence is reproduced here with permission from Really Great Reading: *Phonics Blitz* (Farrell & Hunter, in press).

Exercise 4.5 View a Video Demonstration of a Phonics Lesson Component

(*Teaching Reading Essentials* [Moats & Farrell, 2007], Part 3, Demonstration 7.)

- Use the following checklist to note examples of explicit and systematic teaching in the video. Be ready to discuss your observations.

Observation Checklist for Systematic and Explicit Instruction	
The Teacher . . .	**Examples**
. . . *demonstrates*, or *shows*, students *how* to do something. **"I do"**	
. . . *explains* to students *how* or *why* to do something while demonstrating the skill. **"I do"**	
. . . *breaks down the skill* into simpler steps, *shows*, and *explains* the process or concept to students. **"I do"**	
. . . *provides support* by doing the task with students. **"We do"**	
. . . *provides feedback* through specific praise and immediate correction. **"We do"**	
. . . *slowly releases the responsibility* for students to practice independently. **"You do"**	

The Value of Practice

Often overlooked elements of effective phonics lessons are **practice** and **repetition**. Studies of the repetitions needed for students to automatize new phonic elements help us understand the importance of sounding out words, building words, and reading carefully designed texts with the phonic features we have taught. Learners vary in the number of repetitions they require to automatize new associations, as this chart illustrates.

Type of Learner	Average Number of Repetitions Needed
Most capable	1 or 2
Average	4 to 12
Least capable	20 +

Given these guideposts, one can see how important it is to follow the introduction of a new concept with extended and varied opportunities to practice the new skill. The following exercises present a few instructional tools that are meant to supplement any phonics lessons and provide the extra practice students need through active, hands-on involvement.

Teaching Sound Blending

There are several procedures for teaching sound blending. We will practice the one called *whole-word blending*, or *touch and say*. (Continuous sounds are easier to begin with. For example, /b/ /ă/ /t/ or /ch/ /ĕ/ /k/ are a little harder than /sh/ /ĕ/ /l/, /th/ /ĭ/ /n/, or /m/ /ŏ/ /s/.)

Students touch each letter tile or grapheme, say the sounds as they touch the letter(s), and then blend the whole word together, sweeping their finger across the word. An example of this procedure using the word **wheel** is as follows:

1. Point to the digraph **wh** at the beginning of **wheel**. Say "sound"; students respond "/w/" or "/wh/" (the unvoiced /wh/ is not typical of American English speakers.)
2. Touch each successive grapheme, saying "sound" for each one—/ē/ /l/—as students make the sound the grapheme stands for.
3. Then go back and blend the whole word smoothly—/w/ /ē/ /l/—running your finger under the word left to right.
4. Slowly compress the extended word. Go from *whwheeeelll* to **wheel**.
5. Point to the word and say, "The word is **wheel**."
6. Check for understanding by asking students to use **wheel** in a phrase or sentence.

Exercise 4.6 Practice Sound Blending

- Practice blending with a partner or small group.
- Choose words from each category:
  1. Simple words (no digraphs or blends): **top, bad, net, mud**
  2. Words with digraphs and doubled letters: **moss, shell, thing, whiff**
  3. Words with blends: **stop, shelf, milk, thrift, crash**
- Write the words on a sheet of paper, and take turns being the teacher to practice whole-word sound blending.

Phoneme-Grapheme Mapping

This technique is especially valuable for second and third graders whose phonics and spelling are weak. Developed by Grace (2007), *Phonics and Spelling Through Phoneme-Grapheme Mapping* (PGM) follows a systematic scope and sequence based on the six syllable types and includes word lists for every concept. Sound-spelling boxes can also be used, however, to complement other phonics and spelling programs (e.g., PGM can be used to present a new correspondence within a cumulative sequence). The PGM concept can also be used to explain to students why words are spelled the way they are and to give corrective feedback when misspellings occur. PGM is especially useful when second- and third-grade students:

- need a novel, multisensory technique that will engage their attention;
- are learning that one sound can be spelled with more than one letter; or
- need extra practice attending to the details of spelling.

Systematic Steps for Phoneme-Grapheme Mapping

To use this technique, you will need:

- A transparency of the Phoneme-Grapheme Mapping Grid (see p. 119)
- Grid paper or copies of the Phoneme-Grapheme Mapping Grid for students
- Movable markers (e.g., tiles) that will fit in the grid boxes

1. Introduce the PGM concept; model and explain the *sound* or *sound pattern* of the lesson.
   Example:
   - "Today we'll learn that three different sounds are spelled with double letters when they come at the end of a one-syllable word."
   - "Say **stuff**. What's the last sound you feel as you say that word? Yes, it's /f/."
   - "Say **mill**. What's the last sound in that word? Yes, it's /l/."
   - "Say **pass**. What's the last sound in that word? Yes, it's /s/."
   - "The sounds /f/, /l/, and /s/ are usually spelled with doubled letters at the end of one-syllable words."
2. Using an overhead projector, point to a row of boxes on the grid. Tell students they will segment words into phonemes by placing one tile for each speech sound in a grid box.
   Example:
   - "One tile equals one *sound*, not one letter. We'll say the word, and then we'll say each phoneme while we place a tile."
   - "Watch me—**mill**, /m/ /ĭ/ /l/." (Place the tiles in three boxes as you say each phoneme.)
   - "Let's do another one together—**well**, /w/ /ĕ/ /l/." (Students say each sound and place their tiles while you demonstrate on the overhead.)
   - Repeat with the words **Jeff**, **sill**, and **boss**. As students work, ask them questions such as:
     - "What does this tile stand for?"
     - "What tile stands for /l/?"
3. Now show students a list of words that demonstrate the concept you are working on. Ask students to:
   a. Read the word list silently, then together.
   b. Circle the doubled letters at the end of each word.

shall	shell	dull	doll	still
stuff	whiff	staff	cliff	scoff
grass	chess	kiss	Bess	muss

4. Turn attention to the Phoneme-Grapheme Mapping Grid.
   - "We are going to see how the *sounds* (phonemes) in a word map to its *letters* (graphemes). Look at your grid paper. We'll use one box for the letter or letters (grapheme[s]) that correspond to each speech sound (phoneme) in a word. *You'll always have the same number of boxes as you have sounds in the word.*"
   - Say a word. Say its sounds as you place a tile in a grid box.
   - Say the sound the first tile represents. Now, slide the tile above the box, and write the grapheme that spells that sound.
   - Say the sound the second tile represents. Now, slide the tile above the box, and write the grapheme that spells that sound.
   - Continue with all the sounds. As students work, ask them questions such as:
     – "What do you hear?"
     – "What do you write?"
   - Read the whole word that was written, blending the sounds left to right, if necessary.

shell	sh	e	ll	
mess	m	e	ss	
stuff	s	t	u	ff
grass	g	r	a	ss

5. Ask students to summarize the mapping concept in their own words (e.g., "A box stands for one phoneme. Two letters are used to spell some sounds. The letters f, l, and s are often doubled at the end of one-syllable words").
6. Practice reading and writing words with the target sound-spelling pattern and those already learned. (Appropriate sentence dictations and decodable text should be used as necessary to reinforce recognition of the patterns.)

Phoneme-Grapheme Mapping

(A Method for Bridging Sound to Print)

Name: ______________________________ Date: ____________________

(Grace, 2007, p. 290)

Exercise 4.7 Spelling Chains With Grapheme Tiles

- Spelling chains require students to compare spoken words carefully and to recognize when words differ by just one phoneme. Spelling chains also provide extra practice with sound-spelling association. This exercise uses grapheme tiles for the chaining activity. Remember, graphemes may be more than one letter (e.g., /th/ is on one tile because it represents one sound).

Part 1

- As an example, you might use the following activity to reinforce the two spellings for the sound /ng/—**ng** (**sing**) and **n** (**sin**k). Words for spelling chains may be taken from a phonics lesson or from a core reading program, but successive words in the chain must differ from each other *by only one sound.*
- Create the following grapheme tiles on sticky notes. Place them in a row above your work surface.

o l th ng n i k b s

- As your instructor dictates words, use the tiles to show the changes in a word's spelling. Be ready to say, "Out comes the [grapheme that is being changed] and in goes the [grapheme that is being substituted]."
  - When is /ng/ spelled **ng**, and when is it spelled with a single **n**?

____

____

Part 2

- Now, work with a partner to develop a new spelling chain of five or six words that will contrast short **i** and long **e** vowel sounds. (Remember—change *only one sound* each time! You may use a nonsense word in your chain if you need to.)
- Pretend that your students know how to decode the most common consonant sounds, including common digraph spellings. You want them to contrast short **i** (spelled with a single **i**) and long **e** (spelled **ee** or **ea**).

____

____

____

____

____

____

____

High-Frequency, Irregular (Heart), and Sight Words

High-frequency words are those that are most commonly used in written English text. In fact, approximately only 100 words account for 50 percent of the words used in print. **Irregular (heart)** words, on the other hand, are those that do not follow phonic patterns. The spellings of about three-fourths of our most frequently occurring words are regular, or pattern-based, while only about one-fourth are truly irregular. We call them "heart" words because they must be learned "by heart."

Sight words are not necessarily irregular words. Sight words are those that students must or can recognize and read automatically *without having to sound them out*. It is important that teachers understand that far fewer words must be memorized "by heart" because of their irregular spellings than most of us think! Consider the spellings of these words. Which ones are truly irregular? Why?

about of water best saw were

Exercise 4.8 Recognizing Heart Words

- Heart words are those that are irregular and must be learned a different way.
- Read this story with a partner. Many of the high-frequency words are underlined in the story. List the heart words that are truly irregular.

____

____

____

____

The Funny Little Bird

By Deborah Glaser

<u>Once</u> <u>upon</u> <u>a</u> <u>time</u>, <u>there</u> <u>was</u> a <u>small</u> <u>pretty</u> bird <u>who</u> <u>could</u> <u>not</u> <u>fly</u>. Her wings <u>would</u> not <u>work</u> right <u>because</u> they were not <u>very</u> <u>big</u>. <u>She</u> had to <u>walk</u>, <u>run</u>, and <u>jump</u> <u>everywhere</u> she <u>went</u>.

"<u>I</u> <u>will</u> <u>not</u> <u>live</u> <u>long</u> if I cannot make my wings go. I <u>know</u> there is a big brown and <u>yellow</u> cat who likes to <u>pick</u> <u>on</u> <u>little</u> birds and <u>carry</u> them <u>around</u> to <u>eat</u> for lunch. I wish I could fly."

But the bird had a gift. She was funny. She told jokes that made <u>people</u> <u>laugh</u>. Once she said, "<u>What</u> is <u>black</u> and <u>white</u> and <u>red</u> <u>all</u> <u>over</u>?" <u>They</u> did not <u>say</u>. It was a puzzle to them.

She said, "A newspaper!"

And that made her friends smile.

<u>One</u> cold night, the bird went to <u>sleep</u> <u>under</u> <u>an</u> <u>old</u> <u>green</u> tree by <u>some</u> <u>water</u> <u>where</u> she could <u>keep</u> <u>warm</u>. When she was sleeping, the brown and <u>yellow</u> cat came <u>around</u>. It <u>saw</u> the bird.

"I do <u>want</u> that <u>small</u> bird! I <u>will</u> <u>not</u> have to <u>work</u> hard to get it."

(continued)

Exercise 4.8 (continued)

"Give me some time," said the small bird. "Please hold those claws. Look here. If I can make you laugh, you will not eat me."

The cat said, "I think I shall wait and see what you say."

The bird said, "Knock, knock."

"Who is there?"

"Iguana."

"Iguana who?"

"Iguana fly away right now!"

She put both of her wings together above her head and gave a hard push. "These wings will help me go so fast now!"

Just when the cat was about to open its mouth, the little bird began to fly. She went up into the tree.

The cat said, "I have been tricked! I don't think that your joke was funny at all."

So the happy bird sat in her own tree, and many could hear her sing for a long time. She was full of pride in her new talent—flying!

- Compare your selection of irregular heart words with your partner's.
  - How do the words compare?
  - Why are the words you chose irregular?
  - Are some really pattern-based?

Exercise 4.9 View a Video Demonstration of a Teacher Teaching a Heart Word

(*Teaching Reading Essentials* [Moats & Farrell, 2007], Part 3, Demonstration 1)

- As you watch the video, note the steps the teacher uses to provide ample exposure to the spelling of an irregular heart word:
    1. The teacher spells the word with letter tiles.
    2. Students take a mental picture of the word.
    3. The teacher turns over the letter tiles.
    4. Students name letters from memory, first in random order, then backward, then in correct sequence.
    5. Students write the word on their boards.
    6. The teacher turns over the letter tiles so that students can check their spelling.
- Describe the method the teacher uses to help students create a strong memory in the orthographic processor.

Exercise 4.10 Role-Play Teaching Heart Words

- Choose one irregular heart word in "The Funny Little Bird" story in Exercise 4.8.
- Teach the word to a partner using the heart-word process demonstrated in the Exercise 4.9 video.

Exercise 4.11 Phoneme Awareness or Phonics: Which One Is It?

- Write "PA" (for phoneme awareness) on one index card and "Phonics" on another.
- Listen to the sample teaching prompts or questions, and hold up the card that indicates which component of instruction is being addressed. (Hint: Does the task ask for *sounds* or *letters*?)

1. How many speech sounds are in the word **bat**?
2. Sound out this written word: **rug**.
3. What silent letter is at the end of **game**?
4. Listen: /f/ /r/ /ŏ/ /g/. What is the word?
5. What letter spells the sound /s/ when followed by **i**, **e**, **y**?
6. Spell a word with more than 10 letters.
7. Tap out the speech sounds in **lake**.
8. Tell me the middle sound in **mom**.
9. Find a word that ends with **-ll**.
10. Say **bed** without the /b/.
11. What two letters spell the sound /sh/?
12. Spell the first syllable in **cracker**.
13. Change the /ŏ/ in **cop** to /ă/. What's the new word?

Take 2 Review

- Complete this two-column organizer.
- In the first column are restatements of main ideas. Work with the group or a partner to complete the second column. List a few details that elaborate the main ideas or that state the relevance of those ideas for your school or classroom.

Knowledge/Main Ideas	Application/Practice
1. Explicit and systematic phonics instruction results in higher levels of reading comprehension for greater numbers of students.	
2. Practice is critical to support mastery and automatic application of the alphabetic principle to reading and spelling.	

Linking Concepts to Your Core Program

- Which patterns are taught or reviewed in your program?
- Do you have sound-spelling cards?
- What are some instructional strategies used to introduce the patterns?
- Are any spelling rules taught (e.g., doubling, dropping, or changing)?

What Else Goes Into Word Study?

Once students have become automatic with the basic phonic principles, including the common and not-so-common phoneme-grapheme correspondences, they are ready for *advanced word analysis*. In well-designed reading programs, phonics instruction continues beyond simple phoneme-grapheme correspondence to include analysis at the morpheme and syllable levels. The student of sound-symbol relationships graduates to decoding multisyllabic words and then to the morpheme or meaning level. Advanced word analysis picks up where many practitioners think phonics instruction stops, and the tools students learn in advanced word analysis become the tools they will use to read unfamiliar words, spell them, and decipher meaning at the word level for the rest of their lives.

What Else Is There to Learn About Phonics, Spelling, and Word Study?

These topics are addressed in more depth in LETRS *Modules 3*, 7, and *10* (Moats, 2004c, 2004g, 2004j):

- How word history influences spelling patterns
- Why and how English spelling reflects both sound and meaning
- Advanced phoneme-grapheme mapping
- Position-based spellings in English, such as **-ck**, **-tch**, and **-dge**
- Principles and techniques for dividing multisyllabic words
- Six syllable types in English
- Word endings and how they affect spelling
- Morphemes: what they are and how to teach them
- Distinguishing syllables and morphemes

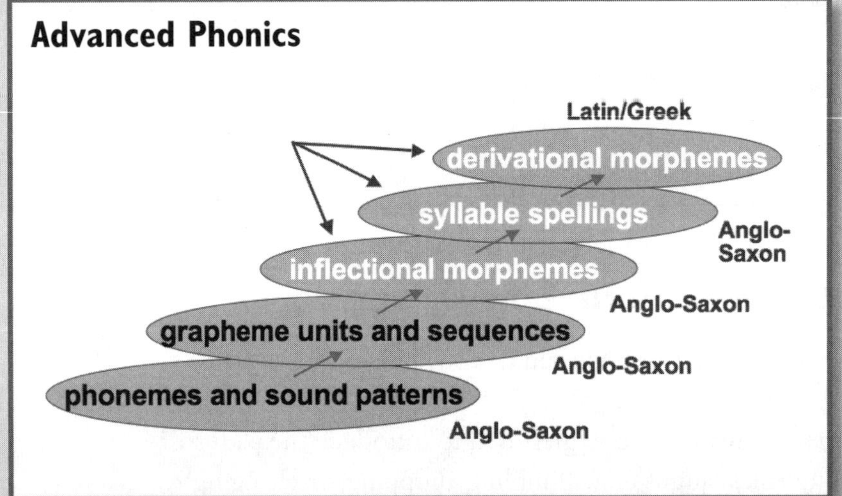

- Advanced phonics instruction will cover much more than phoneme-grapheme correspondences. Word study continues beyond phoneme-grapheme relationships to syllable types, and decoding meaningful units such as inflectional and derivational morphemes.
- Instruction in morphology will occur once students have the building blocks.

What Else Is There to Learn About Phonics, Spelling, and Word Study? (continued)

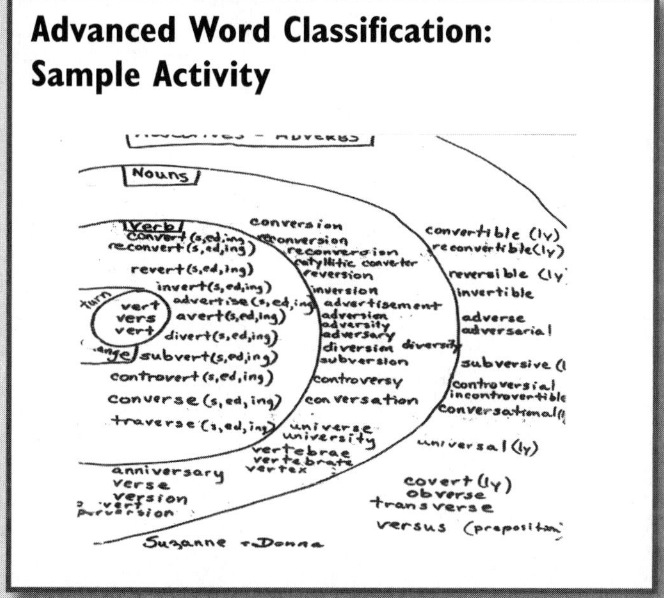

- Advanced phonics and word study will involve activities such as classifying words that come from the Latin root *vers*, *vert*.
- LETRS *Module 10* addresses morphology in depth.
- There is lots more to know than what we have covered in LETRS *Foundations*!

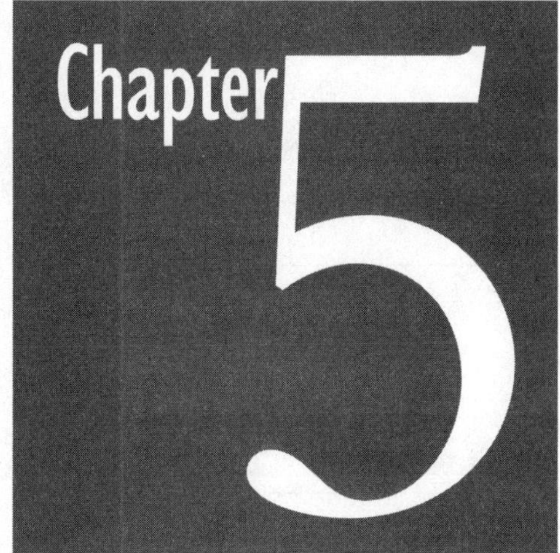

Chapter 5 Reading Fluency

Learner Objectives for Chapter 5

- Define reading fluency.
- Understand the contributing role of automaticity to fluent reading.
- Know how fluency is assessed.
- Understand how fluency is related to other major components.
- Learn how to provide fluency training through timed repeated readings.
- Learn how to organize partner reading.
- Define what **monitored oral reading practice** is and explain the importance of providing multiple opportunities to read text.
- Understand a framework for assessing students' instructional needs.

Warm-Up Activity and Questions

- Watch the video clip from *Teaching Reading Essentials* (Moats & Farrell, 2007) and listen carefully to the students' reading.
- Answer the following questions and be ready to discuss reading fluency.

1. What is *reading* fluency?

   ____

   ____

2. What does a fluent reader sound like?

   ____

   ____

3. What enables a person to be a fluent reader?

   ____

   ____

4. What is your definition of *fluent reading*?

____

____

Defining and Understanding Reading Fluency

What Is Reading Fluency?

Most educators consider the answer to this question to be pretty straightforward because the observable behaviors of fluent reading are easy to recognize. Fluent reading is smooth, fluid, and more enjoyable to listen to than the choppy, slow, and tentative reading of the dysfluent reader. Fluent readers read words accurately and comprehend what they are reading, so they read with *prosody*, or phrasing and expression. Fluent readers sound as if they understand what they are reading. Fluent reading communicates the meaning of the text; as we listen, we can make sense of the passage.

Qualitative measurement of reading fluency, accomplished by rating such features as smoothness and expression, is possible, but reliability of such rating scales is somewhat difficult to achieve. A more objective or quantitative method of judging reading fluency is necessary for judging student progress and for judging whether a student is at the expected level for his or her grade. For this reason, we quantify reading fluency by measuring the additional characteristics of *rate* and *accuracy*. Reading fluency can be measured and monitored by counting the number of words read correctly per minute in a one-minute passage. The statistic that is valid and reliable for assessing fluency is *words correct per minute* (WCPM). Researchers have established norms to determine expected levels of reading fluency in grades 1–8, shared later in this chapter. Simple, one-minute samples of oral reading *rate* and *accuracy* with standardized passages are reliable and valid measures of reading proficiency.

What Is Automaticity?

What is it that enables the fluent, proficient, and seemingly effortless application of a skill such as reading or any other high-performance skill (e.g., skiing, driving, playing a musical instrument)? Revisiting our earlier analogy to musicianship: Why can Eric Clapton perform intricate guitar solos so effortlessly? Why can Itzhak Perlman play a violin concerto from memory? Effortless application of a complex, acquired skill rests on subskills that must be learned to levels of *automaticity*. Subskills become automatic following instruction and lots of practice. Once skills become automatic, conscious application of those skills is no longer needed and attention is freed up for higher-level functions such as creative invention, problem solving, or strategizing. In reading, automatic subskills free up attention for comprehension.

What skills need to be learned to a level of automaticity in order to read fluently and comprehend what is read? The answer lies in the Four-Part Processor and in the menu of language ingredients. Complete the following exercise to determine the subskills that students must learn to automatic levels for fluent reading to occur.

Exercise 5.1 Where Is Fluency in the Four-Part Processor?

- Answer these questions, writing your answers inside the processor ovals as directed.
    1. Label the bottom left oval. What do we teach to strengthen this processor?
    2. Label the bottom right oval. What do we teach to strengthen this processor?
    3. Describe the relationship between processors 1 and 2.
    4. Label the middle oval. What do we teach to strengthen this processor?
        - Through what other experiences is this processor strengthened?
        - What is the relationship between this processor and the subskills below it?
    5. Label the top oval. What do we teach to strengthen this processor?
        - Through what other experiences is this processor strengthened?
        - What is the relationship between this processor and the ones below it?
    6. Where is *fluency*? Fluency is the automatic integration of **all** these skills!

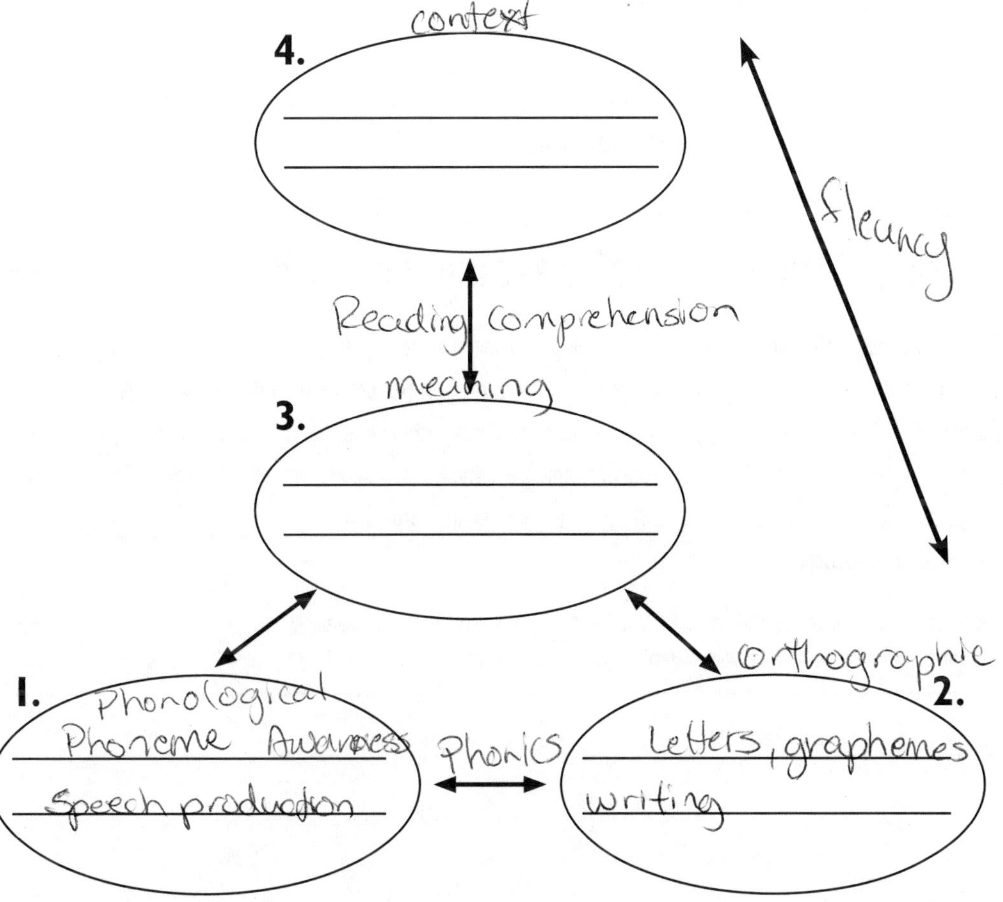

pg. 211

How Do We Teach and Build Fluency?

We teach fluency when we focus students on phoneme awareness, orthographic awareness, decoding, word recognition, sentence comprehension, and passage reading. Reading can be compared to a multi-component machine: optimum performance is dependent on well-oiled parts and efficient operation. Automaticity in word recognition, which is dependent on the subskills of phoneme awareness and decoding, means quick access to the meanings of words on a page. Once words are decoded and their meanings accessed, fluent readers can devote their attention to understanding what they are reading. When students are reading fluently, they usually are comprehending, as well.

We build fluency when we provide lots of opportunities for students to practice reading various kinds of texts that are at an appropriate level of difficulty. It is impossible to be a fluent reader without good word-recognition skills and many hours of reading practice. Students who read more are more fluent readers.

Oral passage reading encompasses and reflects the subskills of decoding, vocabulary, and comprehension. If students are very slow at reading, writing, or language activities, timed exercises to promote fluency will be an important component of a reading or language arts lesson.

Connection With Research

Read the following brief research abstract. Be ready to discuss these questions afterward:

- What is the relationship between reading words per minute (originally referenced as curriculum-based measurement [CBM]) and general reading ability?
- How would you describe the relationship?

Abstract: Study of Oral Reading Fluency*

This study examined the relationship of curriculum-based measurement (CBM), oral reading fluency, to the reading process from a theoretical perspective. It tested reading models (to determine relationships between identified skills and WCPM) using confirmatory factor analysis procedures with 114 third grade and 124 fifth grade students. Subjects were tested on tasks requiring decoding, comprehension, cloze items, written retell, and CBM oral reading fluency. Outcomes demonstrated that CBM oral reading fluency provided a good index of reading proficiency, including comprehension.

* Shinn, M. R., Good, R. H., Knutson, N., Tilly, W. D., & Collins, V. L. (1992). Curriculum-based measurement of oral reading fluency: A confirmatory analysis of its relation to reading. *School Psychology Review, 21*(3), 459–479.

The outcome of this study and others like it helps us understand that reading fluency—as measured by WCPM—is correlated with, and predictive of, decoding and comprehension. In this study, researchers applied statistical analysis to test whether a specified set of measures influences responses in a predictive way and found that WCPM is highly related to many other reading skills.

Measuring Reading Fluency

In order to identify those students who need extra practice in building oral reading fluency or fluency with other reading subskills, we should first assess all students to determine those who are lacking in accurate word-reading skills or those who are accurate but too slow. Not all students need fluency-building exercises; only those who are below par need to spend time on specific exercises. A valid and reliable measure of oral reading fluency will help teachers collect the data in a standardized way and will allow comparison of a student's performance with a grade-level benchmark standard. There are several sets of standardized passages for screening and monitoring student progress within a number of assessments. These are among the most commonly used:

- *Dynamic Indicators of Basic Early Literacy Skills* (DIBELS®) (Good & Kaminski, 2003)
  - Measures and passages for kindergarten through sixth grade
    http://dibels.uoregon.edu or www.sopriswest.com
- AIMSweb® by Edformation
  - Measures and passages for kindergarten through eighth grade
    www.aimsweb.com
- Texas Primary Reading Inventory (TPRI)
  - Screening and inventory measures for all five component areas: phoneme awareness, spelling, word reading, passage reading, and reading comprehension
  - Includes fluency measures
    www.tpri.org
- Read Naturally® Reading Progress Monitor
  - Primary use is for fluency training
  - Includes assessment measures
    www.readnaturally.com

Directions for Administering and Scoring Oral Reading Fluency

Is the measurement of oral reading fluency a one-minute miracle? The deceptively simple one-minute timed measure of oral reading provides robust information about a student's reading ability and takes very little of a teacher's precious instructional time. In one minute, teachers can reliably ascertain a student's reading ability and get a glimpse of his or her decoding and comprehension skills. Although the *one-minute miracle* is only an indicator, it is a powerful predictor of future reading success and a reliable and valid measure when students are being screened for reading problems.

If standardized passages are not available, teachers can still estimate their students' oral reading fluency by using their own grade-level passages and comparing WCPM to the following table of reading performance fluency norms (Hasbrouck & Tindal, 2006). Grade-level text may be found in basal reading programs, reading inventories, and leveled texts.

Note: *Any oral reading fluency measure should be accompanied by a comprehension check, such as students retelling the passage or answering questions about the passage. We do not want students to simply "read for speed."*

Oral Reading Fluency Norms				
		Fall	Winter	Spring
Grade	Percentile	WCPM*	WCPM*	WCPM*
1	90		81	111
	75		47	82
	50		23	53
	25		12	28
	10		6	15
2	90	106	125	142
	75	79	100	117
	50	51	72	89
	25	25	42	61
	10	11	18	31
3	90	128	146	162
	75	99	120	137
	50	71	92	107
	25	44	62	78
	10	21	36	48
4	90	145	166	180
	75	119	139	152
	50	94	112	123
	25	68	87	98
	10	45	61	72
5	90	166	182	194
	75	139	156	168
	50	110	127	139
	25	85	99	109
	10	61	74	83
6	90	177	195	204
	75	153	167	177
	50	127	140	150
	25	98	111	122
	10	68	82	93
7	90	180	192	202
	75	156	165	177
	50	128	136	150
	25	102	109	123
	10	79	88	98
8	90	185	199	199
	75	161	173	177
	50	133	146	151
	25	106	115	124
	10	77	84	97

* WCPM = words correct per minute on grade-level passages
Source: Hasbrouck & Tindal, 2006

Using a passage that has been determined to represent the student's approximate grade level, instruct the student: "Please read this passage out loud. Begin reading here [point], and read until I tell you to stop. If you come to a word you don't know, I will tell you the word." Time the student for one minute and note the number of words he/she reads. Subtract the errors for a total of WCPM.

Reading errors:

- *Unknown word*: The student hesitates or attempts to read a word but does not produce the correct word in three seconds. Provide the correct word for the student, and mark it as an error on your copy of the text.
- *Substitution*: The student misreads a word, substituting a different word for the actual word in the text.
- *Omission*: The student leaves out a word while reading.

Do not count as errors:

- Rereading words or phrases
- Adding words (this can take extra time and will affect score)
- Self-corrections made within three seconds
- Skipping a line (do not count the words in the omitted line as errors; do not count them in the total words read)

Exercise 5.2 Practice Scoring WCPM

- **Look at this passage transcript of a third-grade student reading aloud in January of the school year. The passage is from *The Six-Minute Solution* (Adams & Brown, 2004).**

Moving Waveforms

Sounds are a part of everyday life. Car horns beep. Dogs bark. 12
Children shout. Noisy jets roar across the sky. People whisper to one 24
another. There are hundreds of sounds made every day. It is easy for 37
people to tell them apart. But there are other sounds that cannot be 50
heard by people. These sounds are too high-pitched for the human ear. 63
They are called ultrasounds. 67

Sounds are produced by a certain type of motion. These motions 78
are called vibrations. Sound travels from] a vibrating object to a human ear. 91
It does this by using a sound carrier. The sound carrier may be a solid, 106
liquid, or a gas. One way sound travels is through air. Sound waves 119
make the particles in the air move. One moving particle touches another 131
particle and makes that new particle move. Then that particle touches the 143
next particle and so on. If there is no sound carrier, no sound can be heard. 159

rather than simply crossing out error, try to write it in

Exercise 5.2 (continued)

- Score the results:
  - What was the student's total number of words read? ________
  - Subtract the number of errors: ________
  - Total WCPM: ________
- Compare the score with the Oral Reading Fluency Norms table on p. 135.
- How would you describe this student's reading fluency? Discuss with a partner, and record your answers.

____

____

____

What Can Teachers Do to Improve Reading Fluency?

When students are not reading fluently—as indicated by oral reading fluency measures such as DIBELS or AIMSweb or by a teacher's own assessment—the teacher must first determine whether the student has the prerequisite word-recognition skills to support fluent reading. Diagnostic phonics and word-reading surveys should be used to make that determination. Reading accuracy should precede an emphasis on fluency-building.

When fluency-building is appropriate, several proven practices will improve reading fluency. One of the most dependable practices is straightforward reading of suitably difficult material on a daily basis. Left to themselves, students may not practice enough or may choose an inappropriate (i.e., too difficult) text. We are all familiar with struggling students who choose the thickest and most challenging books during their library visits. Students sometimes strive to join the "library book social club" by carrying around the books that everyone else is reading! Carrying books around is one thing; reading them is another.

The Teacher as Personal Trainer

Students need a personal trainer—a teacher—to guide them through the process of becoming fluent readers (Hasbrouck & Denton, 2005). A personal trainer at a gym assesses an individual's current levels of fitness and then determines appropriate fitness goals. Next, the expert trainer carefully designs a workout routine, beginning with attainable levels of exercise that will gently challenge the individual and, supported by regular progress monitoring, modifies the workout routine as needed to attain the desired results. Likewise, a teacher/trainer assesses students' current reading levels and then carefully chooses texts that will provide practice at the right level, assists during reading, monitors growth, and gradually increases text difficulty as students improve.

Exercise 5.3 The Importance of Text Difficulty

- Experience three levels of text difficulty. Each slide presents the same text content, but the first slide represents 70 percent accuracy, the second slide 80 percent accuracy, and the third slide 90 percent accuracy. After each reading, your comprehension will be assessed.

Discussion:

1. What were your experiences while reading each of the texts?
2. What were your comprehension levels?
3. What are the advantages when students are given instructional-level texts for fluency practice?

The texts used for this activity are included in the Answer Key. Don't peek!

Classroom Connections: Improving Reading Fluency

Prepare students to belong to the "library book social club"—to be able to read those books everybody else is reading—by following these fluency-building instructional practices. Fluency builders are based on practice, practice, and more practice with reading materials that range from letter sounds to isolated words to connected text passages. Fluency-building exercises can be timed or untimed drills; either method requires close teacher monitoring and corrective feedback.

On the following few pages are some sample skill builders for letter naming, phoneme segmentation, orthographic pattern recognition, word reading, sentence comprehension, and text reading. (A skill builder is a fluency drill to practice a skill repeatedly in order to build automaticity.) Students read an appropriate skill builder for one minute, charting their performance over time until a desired rate and accuracy are reached.

Exercise 5.4 Sample Some Fluency Builders for Various Components

- Working with a partner, try these exercises. Alternate roles as student and timekeeper.

PRACTICE PASSAGE 103

Cat Families: It's All Relative

0 Did you know that all cats are related? Small house cats and wild
13 lions belong to the same family. They have a lot of things in common. For
28 example, all cats have long claws. They use these claws to grip and tear.
42 Cats keep their claws sharp by scraping them on rough things like tree
55 trunks. Pet owners give house cats scratching posts to use. All cats walk
68 on their toes. Their heels do not touch the ground. Cats have five toes
82 on each front foot. But their back feet only have four toes. Small pads on
97 cats' feet help them to move quietly. Most cats hunt at night. They have
111 a good sense of smell, sharp hearing, and can see well at night. Cats are
126 graceful animals. They are able to climb and balance themselves very
137 well. Cats are able to run quickly and make great leaps.
148 Cats that live in homes are called house cats. Cats are not as
161 friendly as dogs. But they are neat and need less care than dogs. There
175 are two kinds of house cats. One kind has long hair and the other has
190 short hair. Pet cats should be given a warm, dry box for sleeping. They
204 need two or three meals each day.
211 House cats make very good pets for some people.
220

Total Words Read ______
- Errors ______
= CWPM ______

Practice Passages 73

(Adams & Brown, 2007b, p. 73)

(continued)

Exercise 5.4 (continued)

PRACTICE PASSAGE 812

Archaeology: Digging for Buried Treasure

0 Archaeology is the study of earlier civilizations. Scientists who
9 study early times are called archaeologists. Archaeologists look for
18 artifact clues. Artifacts are manmade objects like pottery or tools.
28 Artifacts provide important information. Sometimes artifacts are found
36 by accident. Other times, artifacts are discovered by excavation. Artifacts
46 can be preserved in sand and ice for many years. For example, treasures
59 found in Egyptian tombs were buried in dry sand. They were found intact
72 thousands of years later! When artifacts are found, they must be cleaned
84 to remove sand or soil. Their exact position must be recorded. Artifacts
96 are photographed so they can be studied. Artifacts provide important
106 clues in helping to understand early humans. The archaeologists try
116 to determine when and why the artifacts were important. They study
127 artifacts to find out about the lives of the people who used them. Artifacts
141 can provide clues as to what earlier people ate and drank. Artifacts can
154 help determine whether ancient people traveled and if they played games.
165 Archaeologists in the United States look for Native American relics.
175 These artifacts help them to learn facts about the Indians who lived
187 before Columbus' time. Archaeologists in other parts of the world have
198 found temples that were covered by a volcanic eruption more than a
210 thousand years ago. Archaeology expeditions are ongoing all over the
220 world. Sometimes governments pay for these expeditions. Sometimes
228 colleges or private foundations absorb the cost. New discoveries are made
239 all over the world every day!
245

Total Words Read ______
– Errors ______
= CWPM ______

(Adams & Brown, 2007c, p. 186)

Exercise 5.4 (continued)

Fluency Graph 1

NAME: ______________________________ CLASS: __________

PARTNER: ______________________________ DATE: __________

Correct Words Per Minute															
200															
195															
190															
185															
180															
175															
170															
165															
160															
155															
150															
145															
140															
135															
130															
125															
120															
115															
110															
105															
100															
95															
90															
85															
80															
75															
70															
65															
60															
55															
50															
45															
40															
35															
30															
25															
20															
15															
10															
5															
DATE															
PASSAGE NUMBER															

290 The Six-Minute Solution: A Reading Fluency Program (Secondary Level)

(Adams & Brown, 2007b, p. 290)

(continued)

Exercise 5.4 (continued)

SET 13

Automatic Word List

0	perhaps	itself	York	it's	times
5	law	human	line	above	name
10	example	action	company	hands	local
15	show	whether	five	history	gave
20	today	either	act	feet	across
25	perhaps	itself	York	it's	times
30	law	human	line	above	name
35	example	action	company	hands	local
40	show	whether	five	history	gave
45	today	either	act	feet	across
50	perhaps	itself	York	it's	times
55	law	human	line	above	name
60	example	action	company	hands	local
65	show	whether	five	history	gave
70	today	either	act	feet	across
75					

Total Words Read ______
\- Errors ______
= CWPM ______

(Adams & Brown, 2007b, p. 239)

Exercise 5.4 (continued)

ONE-MINUTE FLUENCY BUILDER SERIES

SEE TO MARK

Simple Subject and Verb in Sentences

Directions: Underline the simple subject once; the verb twice.

	Correct	Error
First Try		
Second Try		

1. My cousins live in Indianapolis.
2. The swimmers waited for the starting whistle.
3. Nancy played the flute in the band.
4. Almost all the beekeepers wear protective masks.
5. Jamal helped with the rink after school.
6. The two boys built a chicken coop.
7. Lucia caught the fly easily.
8. The copilot radioed the tower.
9. Tall elms lined the avenue.
10. The three girls walked home together.
11. The desktop was uneven.
12. The three boys were cousins.
13. The farmer noticed the vacant stall.
14. Their car is a compact.
15. That CD sounds scratchy.
16. The washing machine had stopped.
17. Kathy had been ready for over an hour.
18. The girls have finished their work.
19. The two ducks were huddling near the pond.
20. Chuck does not like chocolate ice cream.
21. I will endorse this candidate.
22. The workers pushed and shoved with their shoulders.
23. Nisha folded the picture and cut it.
24. Everyone swam, played ball, and then ate a good lunch.
25. Marie and her father skate and ski together.
26. High above our heads stretched the Bay Bridge.
27. Over the housetops roared the wind.
28. Please walk the dog after dinner. you
29. Ling ran through the yard.
30. The kittens wandered around the room.
31. Her teacher read the story to the class.
32. Have you seen that movie yet?
33. Their new car was bright red.
34. The children listened to the music.

Practicing Basic Skills in Language Arts • 221

(Beck, Anderson, & Conrad, 2005, p. 221)

(continued)

Exercise 5.4 (continued)

Letter Name Cumulative Review

1. "Today we practice saying the letter names fast."
   "Hoy vamos a practicar diciendo los nombres de las letras rápidamente."
2. "Point to the letter, and say its name."
   "Señalen la letra y díganme el nombre."
   Make it a game-like format (e.g., "Let's see how many letters you can name in one minute."). (e.g., "Veamos cuántas letras que ustedes pueden nombrar en un minuto.") Attempt to get the children to practice several times.

	r	p	s	b	c
5	w	s	i	o	J
10	D	R	t	P	n
15	B	M	W	T	l
20	H	j	g	r	t
25	p	s	b	g	w
30	A	b	i	j	R
35	H	C	b	P	n
40	a	l	t	w	B
45	n	r	J	O	C
50	b	p	n	i	a

Lesson 20 – Page 381

(Nelson, Cooper, & Gonzalez, 2004, p. 381)

Exercise 5.4 (continued)

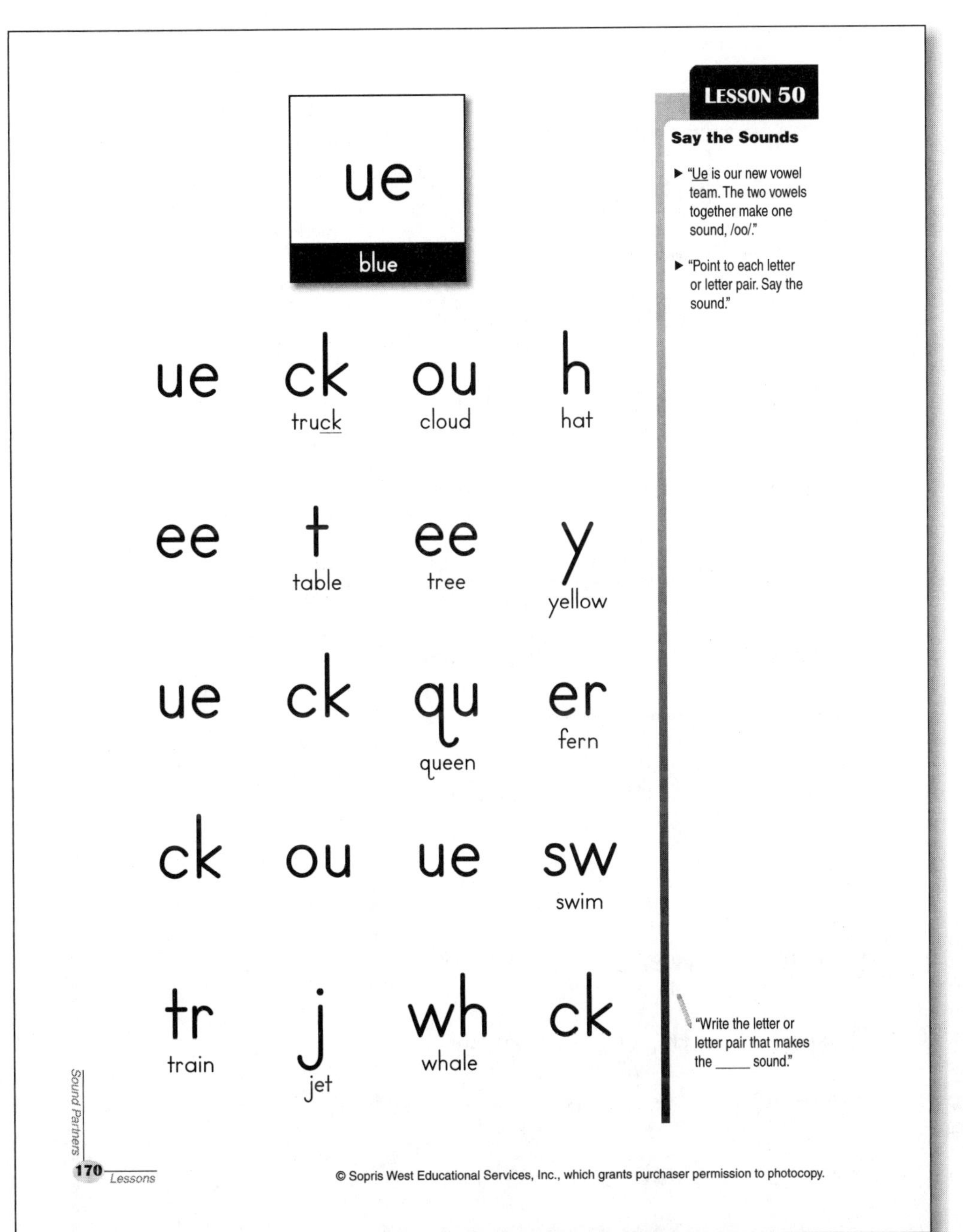

LESSON 50
Say the Sounds
▶ "Ue is our new vowel team. The two vowels together make one sound, /oo/."
▶ "Point to each letter or letter pair. Say the sound."
ue
blue
ue
ck
truck
ou
cloud
h
hat
ee
t
table
ee
tree
y
yellow
ue
ck
qu
queen
er
fern
ck
ou
ue
sw
swim
tr
train
j
jet
wh
whale
ck
"Write the letter or letter pair that makes the _____ sound."
Sound Partners
170 Lessons
© Sopris West Educational Services, Inc., which grants purchaser permission to photocopy.

(Vadasy et al., 2005, p. 170)

(continued)

Exercise 5.4 (continued)

Lesson 50 cont'd

blue

blue	sifter	pouch
coffee	noun	glue
wham	due	sixteen
clue	ground	cloudy
deeper	with	thunder

Word Reading

- "Sound these out and say them fast."

"What sound does ____ **start** with?"

"What sound(s) does ____ **end** with?"

"What is the **middle/ vowel** sound in ____?"

"Now you spell ____."

Choose three words for student to spell and read.

by	she	saw
want	house	my
mouse	were	what
there	they	over

Sight Words

- *Have student read, point and spell, and then reread each word.*

Dictate four sight words for student to spell and read.

Sound Partners Lessons 171

(Vadasy et al., 2005, p. 171)

Exercise 5.5 Reading Nonsense Words

- How well a student reads nonsense words is a good indicator of how well the student knows and uses phonics to recognize new words. While nonsense words are not generally used to *teach* decoding skills, they are a valid and reliable *measure* of decoding skills. If students make errors on nonsense words, they probably need more phonics instruction to improve their word-reading accuracy before they attempt to increase their reading speed.
- Try to read these nonsense syllables. Which ones are you unsure of? Go over them with a partner and/or your trainer.

vog	tel	ut
zek	bux	pef
trum	blesh	splin
gake	pune	lete
tark	yort	mir
soik	zail	shay
quaw	warth	prew

Monitor Oral Reading

Research suggests that teachers should *monitor and assist* students while they are reading to improve their fluency (Stahl, 2004):

- Listen to students read, provide feedback, ask for a retell, and assist with the decoding of unknown or missed words.
- Provide daily and frequent assisted opportunities for students to read orally.

This method appears to increase reading fluency more than unassisted, independent reading.

Text difficulty is a consideration when the goal is to increase levels of reading fluency; however, research does not provide conclusive guidance to help us know which level, easy or difficult, will be most effective in helping students gain reading fluency. At this time, more challenging instructional-level text appears to result in higher gains (Stahl, 2004). If students are not reading at benchmark levels on fluency measures, frequent oral reading of *instructional-level text*, assisted and with repetition (repeated readings of the same text), can help students improve. Be a personal trainer by carefully choosing the text for oral reading and by monitoring the reading process.

Answer these questions and share your answers:

- How will you provide your students with opportunities for extended oral reading practice?

  ____

  ____

  ____

- How will you monitor their reading?

  ____

  ____

  ____

Model Fluent Reading

Read often to students from well-written literature:

- Model expression, hesitations, and inflection as guided by punctuation, content, and phrasing.
- Model comprehension strategies (e.g., rereading) when clarification is needed, probing the context for new word meanings and checking decoding of "unfamiliar" words.
- What's your favorite book to read aloud?

  ____

Repeated Reading

Rereading is necessary only for students whose WCPM is below expectations. Repeated readings can take on many different formats and procedures, but generally any repeated reading technique will direct students to read and reread material three or four times. Remember to monitor and assist during reading!

A repeated-reading formula for **elementary** students who need fluency training might look like this:

DAY I

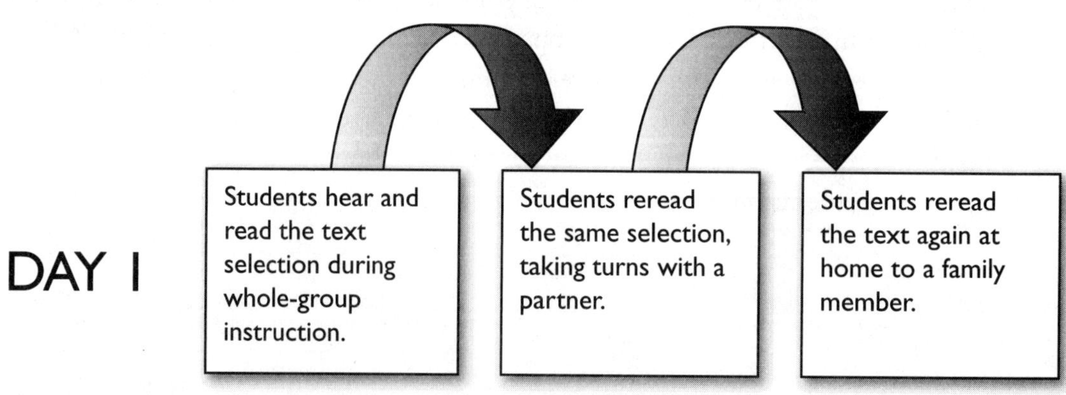

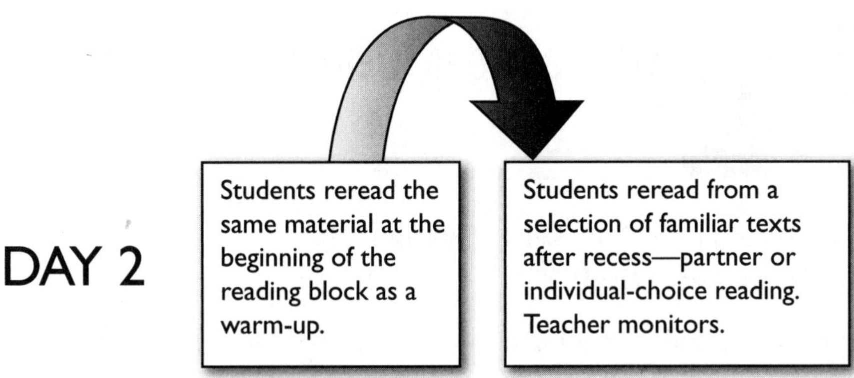

Here is a repeated-reading formula for **intermediate and secondary** students who need fluency training:

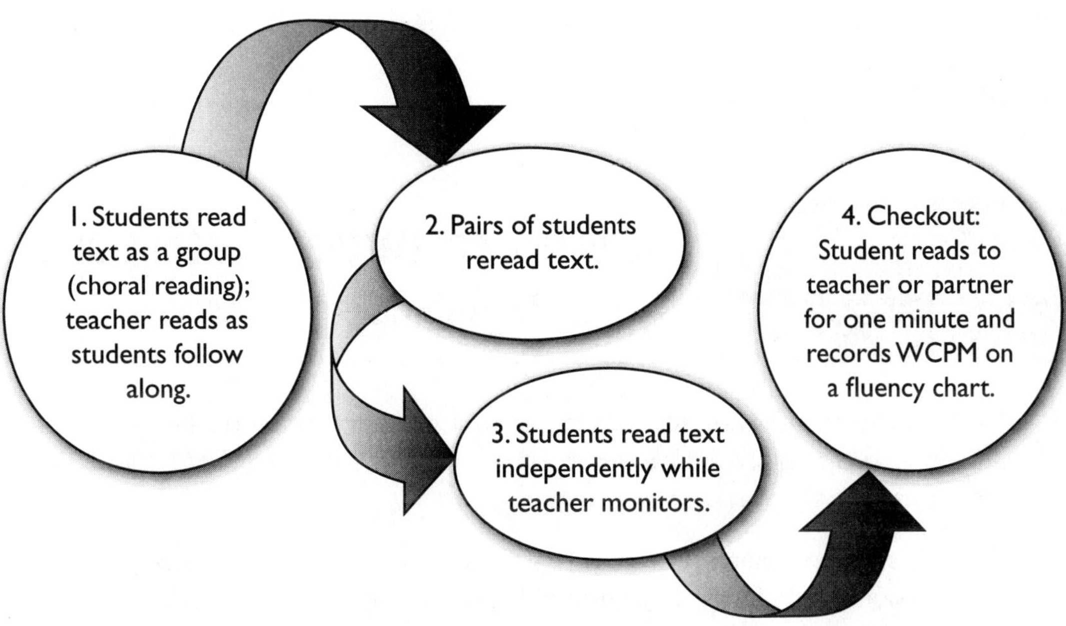

Brainstorm and share other ideas for providing repeated-reading opportunities (all grade levels):

____

____

____

____

____

Reminder: *During monitored independent oral reading, the teacher actively participates by moving around the room, listening and checking for accurate word reading and comprehension through spot checks.*

Exercise 5.6 View a Video Demonstration of Partner Reading

(*Teaching Reading Essentials* [Moats & Farrell, 2007], Part 3, Demonstration 22)
Technique is from Mathes, Torgesen, Allen, & Allor (2001).

- Watch what the teacher does to teach students how to help each other read more fluently.
- Note what happens during the "I Do," "We Do," and "You Do" parts of the lesson:

(I Do) ____

(We Do) ____

(You Do) ____

Exercise 5.7 Research on Partner Reading and Other Techniques

- Many of the previous methods suggested for setting up classroom practice routines included peer partnering as an organizational and management tool. Just what does research say about this practice? What does research tell us about reading prosody?
- Read the following three abstracts, note the findings that are most meaningful to your teaching, and compile a summary of the findings. Be prepared to discuss your thoughts.

Abstract #1 (Stahl & Heubach, 2005)

This paper reports the results of a two-year project designed to reorganize basal reading instruction to stress fluent reading and automatic word recognition. The reorganized reading program had three components: a redesigned basal reading lesson that included repeated reading and partner reading, a choice reading period during the day, and a home reading program. Over two years of program implementation, students made significantly greater-than-expected growth in reading achievement in all fourteen classes. All but two children who entered second grade reading at a primer level or higher (and half of those who did not) were reading at grade level or higher by the end of the year. Growth in fluency and accuracy appeared to be consistent over the whole year. Students' and teachers' attitudes toward the program were positive. In evaluating individual components, we found that self-selected pairs seemed to work best and that children chose partners primarily out of friendship.

Exercise 5.7 (continued)

Children tended to choose books that were at or slightly below their instructional level. In addition, children seemed to benefit instructionally from more difficult materials than generally assumed; this was probably because of the greater amount of scaffolding provided in this program.

Stahl, S. A., & Heubach, K. H. (2005). Fluency-oriented reading instruction. *Journal of Literacy Research, 37*(1), 25–60.

Key points: ______________________________

____

____

____

Abstract #2 (Meisinger, Schwanenflugel, Bradley, & Stahl, 2004)

The influence of social relationships, positive interdependence, and teacher structure on the quality of partner reading interactions was examined. Partner reading, a scripted cooperative learning strategy, is often used in classrooms to promote the development of fluent and automatic reading skills. Forty-three pairs of second grade children were observed during partner reading sessions taking place in twelve classrooms. The degree to which the partners displayed social cooperation (instrumental support, emotional support, and conflict management) and on-task/off-task behavior was evaluated. Children who chose their own partners showed greater social cooperation than children whose partners were selected by teachers. However, when the positive interdependence requirements of the task were not met within the pair (neither child had the skills to provide reading support, or no one needed support), lower levels of on-task behavior were observed. Providing basic partner reading script instruction at the beginning of the year was associated with better social cooperation during partner reading, but providing elaborated instruction or no instruction was associated with poorer social cooperation. It is recommended that teachers provide basic script instruction and allow children to choose their own partners. Additionally, pairings of low-ability children with other low-ability children and high-ability children with other high-ability children should be avoided. Teachers may want to suggest alternate partners for children who inadvertently choose such pairings or adjust the text difficulty to the pair. Overall, partner reading seems to be an enjoyable pedagogical strategy for teaching reading fluency.

Meisinger, E. B., Schwanenflugel, P. J., Bradley, B. A., & Stahl, S. A. (2004). Interaction quality during partner reading. *Journal of Literacy Research, 36*(2), 111–140.

Key points: ______________________________

____

____

____

Continued

Exercise 5.7 (continued)

Abstract #3 (Schwanenflugel, Hamilton, Kuhn, Wisenbaker, & Stahl, 2004)

Prosodic reading, or reading with expression, is considered one of the hallmarks of fluent reading. The major purpose of the study was to learn how reading prosody is related to decoding and reading comprehension skills. Suprasegmental* features of oral reading were measured in second and third grade children (n = 123) and twenty-four adults. Reading comprehension and word decoding skills were assessed ... Two structural equation models found evidence of a relationship between decoding speed and reading prosody as well as decoding speed and comprehension. There was only minimal evidence that prosodic reading was an important mediator of reading comprehension skill.

* Suprasegmental features are vocal effects that extend over more than one sound segment in an utterance, such as pitch, stress, tone, intonation, or juncture pattern. Suprasegmental features are often used for tone, vowel length, and features like nasalization and aspiration.

Schwanenflugel, P. J., Hamilton, A. M., Kuhn, M. R., Wisenbaker, J. M., & Stahl, S. A. (2004). Becoming a fluent reader: Reading skill and prosodic features in the oral reading of young readers. *Journal of Educational Psychology, 96*(1), 119–129.

Key points: ____

Summary Discussion

- How can this research inform and influence decisions made in classrooms?

Monitoring Student Progress

Regular monitoring of student progress provides teachers with the necessary feedback about whether instruction is effective. Several years ago, assessment practices required teachers to wait long periods of time—sometimes until the end of a school year—to learn whether students had made adequate progress. With the advent of reliable and valid fluency measures, teachers can now monitor student progress regularly and frequently, using the results to continually update and target instructional focus.

Progress monitoring informs teachers and tells them when instructional changes need to be made. If progress monitoring indicates that students are not making progress, then instructional methods and materials need to be adjusted to increase the possibility that students will make gains. When students are making progress, teachers can continue with the current instruction knowing that students are responding positively to instruction.

The progress monitoring process is illustrated on the simple fluency chart that follows. Plot the data points. Use the fluency norms found in this section to assist with establishing a target goal for a student's passage-reading fluency. Determine the number of weeks the intervention will continue. Draw an **aim line** on the chart that will connect the current baseline performance with the target WCPM. Then, record the student's WCPM on weekly timed readings.

Example of Oral Reading Fluency Progress Monitoring Graph (Fluency Chart)

WCPM	Week 1 1/30/06	Week 2	Week 3	Week 4	Week 5	Week 6	Week 7	Week 8	Week 9	Week 10
120										
115										
110										
105										
100										
95										
90										
85	●									
80										
75										
70										
65										
Score										

Exercise 5.8 Plotting and Interpreting Oral Reading Fluency Data

- Plot the following progress monitoring WCPM on the preceding Fluency Chart:

Week 1: 80	Week 6: 90
Week 2: 86	Week 7: 93
Week 3: 90	Week 8: 96
Week 4: 93	Week 9: 96
Week 5: 89	Week 10: 102

- This student's baseline data was taken during the winter of third grade. Compare this Fluency Chart with the Oral Reading Fluency Norms table (p. 135) to answer these questions:
  1. What is the student's baseline WCPM? ____________________
  2. What is the student's target WCPM (spring target)? ____________________
     – Connect the baseline data point with the target data point to create the aim line.
  3. How many weeks does the student have to make the target goal? __________
  4. How many words per minute gain does the student need to make each week in order to reach the target goal as outlined on the chart? ____________________
  5. What are some changes in instruction the teacher could make if the student is not making progress toward the target goal (interventions)? ____________________

     ____

     ____

     ____

- Discuss the student's progress with a partner. Be ready to discuss the progress monitoring process with the whole group.

An Assessment and Grouping Framework

Poor readers are not all alike. You now have the conceptual framework to think about differentiating instruction and forming small groups for intervention. Although the majority of students will be distinguished by *level of reading skill*, they may also differ by the *type of problem* they exhibit:

- Almost all poor readers (about 90 percent) are weak in phonics and word recognition. This majority usually needs instruction in all components.
- Most poor readers (70–80 percent) who are weak in phonics have problems with speech-sound awareness (phonology) early in reading development. Some, with severe phonological problems, will need very skilled instruction in phoneme awareness.
- Some poor readers (10–15 percent) have a specific problem developing automatic, fast word reading, even though they may read words accurately. Fluency building will be a stronger focus of their intervention.
- Some poor readers (10–15 percent) can read words accurately but do not comprehend them. This is especially true of ELL and autism-spectrum students, who need focus on many comprehension skills and strategies.
- The majority of poor readers (at least 70 percent) have trouble with three characteristics—word recognition, fluency, and comprehension—in combination, so most supplementary interventions should be comprehensive.

Take 2 Review

- Complete this two-column organizer.
- In the first column are restatements of main ideas. Work with the group or your partner to complete the second column. List a few details that elaborate the main ideas or that state the relevance of those ideas for your school or classroom.

Knowledge/Main Ideas	Application/Practice
1. Several subskills must be learned to automatic levels for fluent reading to occur.	
2. Reading fluency, as measured by WCPM, is related to comprehension skills.	
3. Students need a personal trainer in the form of a teacher who understands the importance of supported practice to build fluency skills.	

Instructional Programs and Resources for Developing Fluency

- *The Six-Minute Solution: A Reading Fluency Program*—Primary Level (Adams & Brown, 2007a); Intermediate Level (Adams & Brown, 2007b); and Secondary Level (Adams & Brown, 2007c)
- *REWARDS: Multisyllabic Word Reading Strategies* (grades 4–12) (Archer, Gleason, & Vachon, 2005); *REWARDS: Mutltisyllabic Word Reading Strategies—Intermediate Level* (grades 4–6) (Archer, Gleason, & Vachon, 2006)
- *Basic Skill Builders* series (www.sopriswest.com)
- *K-PALS* (Mathes, Clancy-Menchetti, & Torgesen, 2001); *First Grade PALS* (Mathes, Torgesen, Allen, & Allor, 2001)
- *Read Naturally* products (www.readnaturally.com)
- *Great Leaps Reading* program (www.greatleaps.com)
- *QuickReads* series (www.pearsonlearning.com)

What Else Is There to Learn About Fluency and Assessment?

These topics are addressed in more depth in LETRS *Module 5, Getting Up to Speed: Developing Fluency* (Moats, 2004e); *Module 8, Assessment for Prevention and Early Intervention* (Moats, 2004h); and *Module 12, Using Assessment to Guide Instruction* (Moats 2004k):

- Several common causes of dysfluency
- How to calculate fluency and to record and chart fluency results
- Role plays and demonstrations of several strategies for fluency building
- Less effective strategies to minimize or avoid
- How to use screening and progress monitoring as a basis for instructional decision making
- Other informal assessments—including spelling errors and writing samples—in the context of case study analysis
- How to pinpoint the needs of at-risk students
- Selecting diagnostic tests that measure phoneme and morpheme awareness, decoding and word analysis, spelling, written composition, reading fluency, and comprehension

Chapter 6

LETRS *Foundations* in the Classroom

Learner Objectives for Chapter 6

- Differentiate between the *content* of instruction and the *routines* or *methods* of instruction (i.e., "what" versus "how")
- Become familiar with *teacher behaviors* that result in higher levels of learning for students
- View a videotaped example of an integrated, comprehensive lesson
- Learn a framework for grouping students by instructional priorities
- Identify priorities for personal growth as a teacher
- Develop an action plan that specifies how teaching will change and how student learning will change
- Understand the importance of continuing professional development and the role of LETRS in that future

Warm-Up Activity

(Story attributed to Dr. Roland Good)

Two young boys are out playing together with one of the boy's dogs. The owner of the dog tells his friend, "I taught my dog to whistle."

The friend looks at the dog and listens. After a few seconds, the friend says, "I don't hear him."

The boy replies, "I said I taught him; I didn't say he learned."

- With a partner, share the connections between this story and your own teaching experiences. What is the point of this story?

Language Ingredients and Teaching Recipes

Effective instruction includes both strong **content** and effective **methodology**. Put differently, teachers must know *what to teach* and *how to teach it.* The "what" (or content) of instruction in reading, in our view, is best described as the combination of the language ingredients explored earlier and the meaning of the concepts embodied in the reading material. The essential components of a reading lesson or program identified by the National Reading Panel (NICHD, 2000) would cover or include this important content.

The content of instruction includes all the concepts about sounds, words, sentences, and discourse that will help a student develop **linguistic awareness** and fluent reading skill. The content of instruction should be organized, coherent, and useful for developing listening, speaking, reading, and writing skills. In addition, the content of the reading material should be well written, intrinsically interesting to students, and linked to a rich curriculum that is aligned with a state's **content learning standards**. As soon as children can read, they should be reading widely from various genres, such as nonfiction narrative, fictional narrative, folk tales and legends, exposition in science and social studies, and poetry.

The "how" part of teaching includes the methods, routines, or activities used in instruction and/or the selection of specific tools for teaching. One model we have found useful for conceptualizing the "how" of teaching is the Four-Part Processing System we explored in Chapter 1. As instructors, our goal is to help students' brains build connections between speech, print, meaning, and context; to do that, we employ methods that are multisensory and strategic.

Sometimes, we focus so much on the mechanics of activities and strategies that we lose sight of the content, purpose, and goals of instruction. Activities and teaching routines have no inherent value other than facilitating instruction of lesson content. For example, saying that "round-robin reading is bad" may or may not be true depending on how many students are in the group and whether they are all paying attention, getting appropriate practice, enjoying the reading and discussion, or showing that they are learning the content and skills. There may be other, more suitable activities that will lead to successful group reading, but any activity's value is determined by its effect: Is learning toward an objective taking place?

Content and Methodology

Exercise 6.1 Sort Items by "What" (content) or "How" (methodology)

- Read through this list of phrases and terminology.
- Decide if the item applies to "what to teach" or "how to teach," then write it under the appropriate column head in the table.

– consonant digraphs
– one-minute timed letter-naming drill
– touch-and-say blending
– sufficient fluency for comprehension
– repeated readings
– verbal sentence extension
– Level Two vocabulary
– vowel-sound isolation
– using a word often in context
– discourse
– pairing a gesture with a sound
– phoneme/grapheme mapping
– letter names
– main idea location
– summarizing from a graphic organizer
– structure of a narrative (story)
– retelling from a storyboard
– decoding
– charting WCPM
– partner-reading

What to Teach (content)	How to Teach (methods, activities)

Reflect on the Exercise

- What is the advantage of a clear priority ("What to Teach") for instruction?
- Have you ever been in the middle of a lesson and lost sight of what you were teaching? How can that be prevented?
- What is the advantage of having a few proven instructional routines, activities, and programs ("How to Teach") in your repertoire?

Three Keys to Teaching Effectively

Some teachers have a gift, an intuitive understanding of how to plan, organize, pace, and deliver instruction all as a seemingly effortless process. How do they do it? What is their secret? We can learn a lot about effective teaching by observing these master teachers; by learning what the research tells us about the most effective combination of teaching methods, knowledge, and materials; and by defining which teacher behaviors result in the most productive student learning.

No doubt, effective teaching is an art and a science. It unites emotion with reason. It depends on empathy and expertise. It is always much more than any single list of vital characteristics.

That said, educational researchers agree that when teachers have a strong handle on the following two-part "keys," their teaching is likely to be high-quality (Kame'enui, Carnine, Dixon, Simmons, & Coyne, 2002; Vaughn & Briggs, 2003).

Key Number 1: Planning + Knowledge

- **Planning**. Planning is necessary for best use of instructional time and for accomplishing differentiated instruction with students at various levels of proficiency. Planning requires familiarity with the instructional programs and tools available, access to good data on current levels of student performance on critical benchmark skills, and access to supplementary tools when necessary.
- **Knowledge**. Effective teachers know how students learn to read, why some students have difficulty, and what must be directly taught. They use this knowledge to set student goals, deliver instruction, and monitor student progress.

Key Number 2: Presentation + Management

- **Presentation: Follow a routine**. Teachers follow instructional routines within a systematic, explicit presentation. Effective routines provide sufficient practice and connect listening, speaking, reading, and writing. "Scripting" is especially helpful for novice teachers.
- **Management: Maximize academic engaged time**. Teachers enable a high rate of student response by minimizing irrelevant talk, using prompts and cues, structuring tasks at the appropriate level of difficulty, and teaching peers to teach one another.

Key Number 3: Instruction + Monitoring

- **I Do.** Teacher models thinking and learning.
- **We Do.** Teacher provides guided learning with feedback (correction) and many opportunities for students to participate.
- **You Do.** Teacher provides occasion for plenty of *practice*, frequent and distributed.

Exercise 6.2 View a Video Demonstration of a Reading Lesson

(*Teaching Reading Essentials* [Moats & Farrell, 2007], Part 3, Demonstration 26)

Use these questions to guide your viewing of a comprehensive 35-minute reading lesson. Identify what this teacher is teaching and how the teacher uses various instructional methods.

- What is the evidence of good planning? ______________________________

  ____

  ____

- What essential components are addressed in this lesson? ______________________________

  ____

  ____

- What content is being taught? ______________________________

  ____

  ____

- What does the teacher do to encourage active student response? ______________________________

  ____

  ____

- How are student attention and behavior managed? ______________________________

  ____

  ____

- Identify a section in which the sequence "I Do, We Do, You Do" occurs. ______________________________

  ____

  ____

Reflect on the Exercise

- Of the teaching behaviors you observed in the exercise video, which ones would you most like to emulate? Are there ways in which you might have improved this lesson?

____

____

____

____

Teacher Self-Evaluation Checklist

Teachers may use this tool to evaluate whether they use teaching procedures that are linked to elevated student learning. The checklist can help teachers answer the following questions: "Which skills do I have a handle on?" and "Which skills do I need to improve?"

Behavior	Examples	Yes/No
Modeling	Did I demonstrate, or *show* students, *how* to do something?	
	Did I *explain* to students how or why to do something, as I demonstrated?	
	Did I break down the skill into simpler steps, and then *show* and *explain* the process or concept to students?	
Specific Praise	Did I *specify the student behavior* in the praise I provided?	
	Did I provide feedback that *isolated the student performance* of skills I was teaching?	
Corrective Feedback	When students made mistakes, did I respond with the following corrective steps:	
	1. *Model* the correct answer or process.	
	2. *Lead* students to repeat the process correctly with me.	
	3. *Test* if students could answer on their own and repeat again (*firm-up*).	
	4. *Check* again for correct response after a brief period (*delayed test*).	

Behavior	Examples	Yes/No
Monitoring	Did I observe student responses carefully and identify students who responded correctly and those who did not or who hesitated?	
	Did I make a note of student weaknesses in order to recheck learning or reteach?	
	If students were reading in pairs or independently, did I briefly check their skills: listen to them, ask them to read isolated words and text, monitor comprehension, provide feedback and praise?	
Scaffolding	Did I anticipate difficulty with a task and provide support through access to previous learning?	
	Did I provide support by doing the task *with* students and then slowly releasing the responsibility for students to do the task independently?	
	Did I guide students to make a connection between what they know and the new learning?	
Pacing	Did I maintain a brisk, lively pace?	
	Did I prompt for student responses several times per minute (i.e., more student voice than teacher voice)?	
	Did I minimize downtime between student responses?	

This chart used with permission of D. Glaser and S. Smartt, *Next Steps: Fluency Measures and Teaching Struggling Students to Read,* in press.

Exercise 6.3 How Will My Teaching Change? How Will My Students' Learning Change?

"Change is the end result of all true learning." —Leo Buscaglia

- LETRS *Foundations* has introduced you to a body of knowledge that has the potential to change your teaching and your students' learning. If this knowledge was truly learned, change will be a natural outcome. Planning for that change is an essential feature of evaluating this professional development.
- Review your notes and summaries from each previous chapter with your team or school partner(s) (e.g., grade-level groups, school groups). Work with your team or partner(s) to develop an action plan to guide future implementation of what you have learned so far. You may use the Action Plan for Change form (following) or develop your own. We include a sample form that lists target actions.
- Small groups/individuals can share their plans with the whole group.

LETRS® *Foundations* Action Plan for Change

Refer to the LETRS *Foundations* content and "Take 2 Review" sections of each chapter.

- How will you KNOW your teaching has changed?
- How will you KNOW your students' learning has changed?
- What assessment or accountability can you build into your routines to help you know that you are implementing new knowledge and practice?

What I Will Continue Doing	What I Learned (Key Knowledge)	Plan for Change in Classroom Practice (How Will I Know?)	Change in Student Learning (How Will I Know?)

This form is adapted from *Evaluating Professional Development* (Guskey, 2000).

SAMPLE

LETRS® *Foundations* Action Plan for Change

Refer to the LETRS *Foundations* content and "Take 2 Review" sections of each chapter.

- How will you KNOW your teaching has changed?
- How will you KNOW your students' learning has changed?
- What assessment or accountability can you build into your routines to help you know that you are implementing new knowledge and practice?

What I Will Continue Doing	What I Learned (Key Knowledge)	Plan for Change in Classroom Practice (How Will I Know?)	Change in Student Learning (How Will I Know?)
I will continue reading orally to my students. **I will continue using daily phoneme segmentation activities with my students' spelling words.**	**Oral language ability is related to many reading skills.**	**I need to increase the amount of oral language interaction in my classroom. I will plan for it in my daily reading lessons during comprehension and writing instruction.** **I will use the four language stimulation techniques listed in Chapter 2.**	**My students will be more involved in class discussions and expand their oral responses.** **I will use the DIBELS Word Use Fluency assessment as a benchmark assessment to determine if my students are increasing their vocabulary and length of oral responses.**

This form is adapted from *Evaluating Professional Development* (Guskey, 2000).

Into the Future

You have just completed introductory training, the tip of the reading iceberg. Your newly acquired knowledge and plan of action are only a beginning. Change is systemic. To achieve the best student outcomes, a whole school must recognize and attend to the dynamic elements that work together to support change: reading curriculum and materials, school organization, assessment, leadership and support resources, and ongoing professional development.

LETRS *Foundations* is a *link* to future and deeper-level examination of the research and the components of effective, research-based teaching. We hope you will go on to study all of these concepts in greater depth, because teaching reading *is* rocket science!

What Else Is There to Learn?

- Exploring in depth how the brain processes information to learn to read
- Distinguishing student needs on the basis of scientifically grounded concepts
- Using and interpreting screening and progress-monitoring assessments
- Using and interpreting surveys of specific reading and writing skills
- Determining if students are responding to instruction; changing course if necessary
- Supplementing the core, comprehensive program with research-based programs and practices
- Reading assessment and instruction for young students and older students
- Implementing a multitiered approach
- Weaving the components of reading instruction together into a systematic and explicit lesson

Additional LETRS Professional Development Options

In addition to, and supportive of, training with the 12 LETRS modules, a complement of interactive CDs provides modeling, animations, and interactive review exercises to make the most difficult reading, spelling, writing, and assessment topics easy to understand. The CD format allows teachers to study independently or with study groups at schools. The interactive CDs are available with these LETRS modules:

- Module 2, *The Speech Sounds of English: Phonetics, Phonology, and Phoneme Awareness* (Moats, 2004b)
- Module 3, *Spellography for Teachers: How English Spelling Works* (Moats, 2004c)
- Module 4, *The Mighty Word: Building Vocabulary and Oral Language* (Moats, 2004d)
- Module 7, *Teaching Phonics, Word Study, and the Alphabetic Principle* (Moats, 2004g)
- Module 8, *Assessment for Prevention and Early Intervention* (Moats, 2004h)

Bibliography

Adams, G., & Brown, S. (2004). *The six-minute solution: A reading fluency program* (1st ed.). Longmont, CO: Sopris West Educational Services.

Adams, G., & Brown, S. (2007a). *The six-minute solution: A reading fluency program (primary level).* Longmont, CO: Sopris West Educational Services.

Adams, G., & Brown, S. (2007b). *The six-minute solution: A reading fluency program (intermediate level).* Longmont, CO: Sopris West Educational Services.

Adams, G., & Brown, S. (2007c). *The six-minute solution: A reading fluency program (secondary level).* Longmont, CO: Sopris West Educational Services.

Adams, M. (1990). *Beginning to read: Thinking and learning about print.* Cambridge, MA: MIT Press.

Adams, M. J., Foorman, B. R., Lundberg, I., & Beeler, T. (1998a). The elusive phoneme. *American Educator, 22,* 18–29.

Adams, M. J., Foorman, B.R., Lundberg, I., & Beeler, T. (1998b). *Phonemic awareness in young children: A classroom curriculum.* Baltimore: Paul H. Brookes.

Alcott, L. M. (1996; originally published 1868). *Little women.* New York: Oxford University Press.

Anderson, R. C., Hiebert, E. H., Scott, J. A., & Wilkinson, I. A. G. (1985). *Becoming a nation of readers: The report of the commission on reading.* Champaign, IL: Center for the Study of Reading and the National Academy of Education.

Archer, A., Gleason, M., & Vachon, V. (2000). *Reading excellence: Word attack and rate development strategies* (REWARDS). Longmont, CO: Sopris West Educational Services.

Archer, A., Gleason, M., & Vachon, V. (2005). *Reading excellence: Word attack and rate development strategies* (REWARDS): *Multisyllabic word reading strategies* (grades 4–12). Longmont, CO: Sopris West Educational Services.

Archer, A., Gleason, M., & Vachon, V. (2006). *Reading excellence: Word attack and rate development strategies* (REWARDS): *Multisyllabic word reading strategies— Intermediate level* (grades 4–6). Longmont, CO: Sopris West Educational Services.

Arguelles, M., & Baker, S. (in press). *Teaching English language learners: A supplementary LETRS module.* Longmont, CO: Sopris West Educational Services.

Armbruster, B., Lehr, F., & Osborn, J. (2001). Put reading first: The research building blocks for teaching children to read, kindergarten through grade 3. Washington, DC: National Institute for Literacy.

Atwater, R., & Atwater, F. (1992; originally published 1938). *Mr. Popper's penguins.* New York: Little, Brown Young Readers.

Ayres, J. (1972). Improving academic scores through sensory integration. *Journal of learning disabilities, 5*(6), 338–343.

Balmuth, M. (1992). *The roots of phonics.* Baltimore: York Press.

Bauman, J. F., & Kame'enui, E. (2004). *Vocabulary instruction: Research to practice.* New York: Guilford.

Beck, I. L., McKeown, M. G., & Kucan, L. (2002). *Bringing words to life: Robust vocabulary instruction.* New York: Guilford.

Beck, R., Anderson, P., & Conrad, A. D. (2005). *Practicing basic skills in language arts: One-minute fluency builders series.* Longmont, CO: Sopris West Educational Services.

Blachman, B. A., Ball, E., Black, R., & Tangel, D. (2000). *Road to the code: A phonological awareness program for young children.* Baltimore: Paul H. Brookes.

Blachowicz, C. L., & Fisher, P. (2001). *Teaching vocabulary in all classrooms* (2nd ed.). Upper Saddle River, NJ: Pearson Education.

Carlisle, J. (2004). Morphological processes that influence learning to read. In A. C. Stone, E. R. Silliman, B. J. Ehren, & K. Apel (Eds.), *Handbook of language and literacy: Development and disorders* (pp. 318–339). New York: Guilford.

Carlisle, J. F., Schilling, S. G., Scott, S. E., & Zeng, J. (2004). *Do fluency measures predict reading achievement? Results from the 2002–2003 school year in Michigan's Reading First schools* (Tech. Rep. No.1: Evaluation of Reading First in Michigan). Ann Arbor: University of Michigan.

Chall, J. S. (1967). *Learning to read: The great debate.* New York: McGraw Hill.

Chall, J. S. (1983). *Stages of reading development.* New York: McGraw-Hill.

Chapman, J. W., Tunmer, W. E., & Prochnow, J. E. (2001). Does success in the Reading Recovery program depend on developing proficiency in phonological processing skills? A longitudinal study in a whole-language instructional context. *Scientific Studies in Reading, 5,* 141–176.

Christenson, C. A., & Bowey, J. A. (2005). The efficacy of orthographic rime, grapheme-phoneme correspondence, and implicit phonics approaches to teaching decoding skills. *Scientific Studies of Reading, 9*(4), 327–349.

Committee on the Prevention of Reading Difficulties in Young Children. (1998). *Preventing reading difficulties in young children.* Washington, DC: National Academy of Sciences, National Research Council.

Cunningham, A. E., & Stanovich, K. E. (1998). What reading does for the mind. *American Educator, 22,* 8–15.

Doyle, A. C. (2002; originally published 1902). *The hound of the Baskervilles.* New York: Modern Library.

Ehri, L. C. (1998). Grapheme-phoneme knowledge is essential for learning to read words in English. In J. L. Matsala & L. C. Ehri (Eds.), *Word recognition in beginning literacy* (pp. 3–40). Mahwah, NJ: Erlbaum.

Ehri, L. C. (2004). Teaching phonemic awareness and phonics: An explanation of the national reading panel meta-analysis. In P. McCardle & V. Chhabra (Eds.), *The voice of evidence in reading research* (pp. 153–186). Baltimore: Paul H. Brookes.

Ehri, L., & Snowling, M. (2004). Developmental variation in word recognition. In A. C. Stone, E. R. Silliman, B. J. Ehren, & K. Apel (Eds.), *Handbook of language and literacy: Development and disorders* (pp. 443–460). New York: Guilford.

Farrell, L., & Hunter, M. (in press). *Phonics blitz.* Cabin John, MD: Really Great Reading.

Flesch, R. (1955). *Why Johnny can't read.* New York: Harper Collins.

Fletcher, J., Denton, C., Fuchs, L., & Vaughn, S. (2005). Multi-tiered reading instruction: Linking general education and special education. In S. Richardson & J. Gilger (Eds.), *Research-based education and intervention: What we need to know* (pp. 21–43). Baltimore: International Dyslexia Association.

Fletcher, J., Lyon, G. R., Fuchs, L., & Barnes, M.A. (2007). *Learning disabilities: From identification to intervention.* New York: Guilford.

Foorman, B. R., & Moats, L. C. (2004). Conditions for sustaining research-based practices in early reading instruction. *Remedial and Special Education, 25*(1), 51–60.

Foorman, B. R., & Schatschneider, C. (2003). Measuring teaching practice during reading/language arts instruction and its relation to student achievement. In S. Vaughn (Ed.), *Reading in the classroom: Systems for observing teaching and learning* (pp. 1–30). Baltimore: Paul H. Brookes.

Fromkin, V., & Rodman, R. (1998). *An introduction to language* (6th ed.). Orlando, FL: Harcourt Brace & Co.

Frostig, M. (1965). Corrective reading in the classroom. *The Reading Teacher, 18,* 573–580.

Fuchs, D., & Fuchs, L. S. (2006). Introduction to response to intervention: What, why, and how valid is it? *Reading Research Quarterly, 41,* 93–99.

Fuchs, L. S., Fuchs, D., Hosp, M. K., & Jenkins, J. R. (2001). Oral reading fluency as an indicator of reading competence: A theoretical, empirical, and historical analysis. *Scientific Studies of Reading, 5,* 239–256.

Fry, E. B., Kress, J. E., & Fountoukidis, D. L. (2000). *The reading teacher's book of lists with CD-ROM* (4th ed.). San Francisco: Jossey-Bass.

Gillon, G. T. (2004). *Phonological awareness: From research to practice.* New York: Guilford.

Glaser, D. (2005). *ParaReading: A training guide for tutors.* Longmont, CO: Sopris West Educational Services.

Glaser, D., & Smartt, S. (2006). *Next steps: Fluency measures and teaching struggling students to read.* Self-published manuscript. Author e-mail: smsmartt@comcast.net

Good, R. H., & Kaminski, R. (2003). *Dynamic indicators of basic early literacy skills* (DIBELS®). Longmont, CO: Sopris West Educational Services.

Good, R. H., Simmons, D. C., & Kame'enui, E. J. (2001). The importance and decision-making utility of a continuum of fluency-based indicators of foundational reading skills for third-grade high-stakes outcomes. *Scientific Studies of Reading, 5*(3), 257–288.

Grace, K. (2007). *Phonics and spelling through phoneme-grapheme mapping.* Longmont, CO: Sopris West Educational Services.

Graves, M. F. (2006). *The vocabulary book: Learning and instruction.* New York: Columbia Teachers College Press.

Guskey, T. R. (2000). *Evaluating professional development.* Thousand Oaks, CA: Corwin Press.

Hanna, P. R., Hanna, J. S., Hodges, R. E., & Rudorf, E. H. (1966). *Phoneme-grapheme correspondences as cues to spelling improvement.* Washington, DC: U.S. Government Printing Office.

Hart, B., & Risley, T. R. (1995). *Meaningful differences in the everyday experience of young American children.* Baltimore: Paul H. Brookes.

Hart Paulson, L. (in press). *Early childhood LETRS*. Longmont, CO: Sopris West Educational Services.

Hasbrouck, J., & Denton, C. (2005). *The reading coach: A how-to manual for success*. Longmont, CO: Sopris West Educational Services.

Hasbrouck, J., Denton, C., & Tolman, C. (in press). *The reading coach presenter's kit*. Longmont, CO: Sopris West Educational Services.

Hasbrouck, J., & Tindal, G. A. (2006). Oral reading fluency norms: A valuable assessment tool for reading teachers. *The Reading Teacher, 59*(7), 636–644.

Iverson, S., & Tunmer, W. E. (1993). Phonological processing skills and the Reading Recovery program. *Journal of Educational Psychology, 85*, 112–120.

Jenkins, J. R., Fuchs, L. S., vanden Broek, P., Espin, C., & Deno, S. L. (2003). Sources of individual difference in reading comprehension and reading fluency. *Journal of Educational Psychology, 95*, 719–729.

Jenkins, J. R., Stein, M. L., & Wysocki, K. (1984). Learning vocabulary through reading. *American Educational Research Journal, 21*(4), 767–787.

Justice, L. (2004, November/December). A team-based action plan for creating language-rich preschool classroom environments. *Exceptional Children*, 2–10.

Kaderavek, J., & Sulzby E. (1998). Parent-child joint book reading: An observational protocol for young children. *American Journal of Speech-Language Pathology*, 7(1), 33–47.

Kame'enui, E. J., Carnine, D. W., Dixon, R. C., Simmons, D. C., & Coyne, M. D. (2002). *Effective teaching strategies that accommodate diverse learners*. Upper Saddle River, NJ: Merrill Prentice Hall.

Katzir, T., Kim, Y., Wolf, M., O'Brien, B., Kennedy, B., Lovett, M., et al. (2006). Reading fluency: The whole is more than the parts. *Annals of Dyslexia, 56*(1), 51–82.

Kephart, N. C. (1960). *The slow learner in the classroom*. Columbus, OH: Charles Merrill.

King, R., & Torgesen, J. K. (2006). Improving the effectiveness of reading instruction in one elementary school: A description of the process. In P. Blaunstein & R. Lyon (Eds.), *It doesn't have to be this way*. Lanham, MD: Scarecrow Press.

Learning First Alliance. (2000). *Every child reading: A professional development guide*. Washington, DC: Author.

Liberman, I. Y., Shankweiler, D., & Liberman, A. M. (1989). The alphabetic principle and learning to read. In D. Shankweiler & I. Liberman (Eds.), *Phonology and reading disability: Solving the reading puzzle* (pp. 1–33). Ann Arbor: University of Michigan Press.

London, J. (2005; originally published 1903). *The call of the wild.* Bel Air, CA: Prestwick House.

Mathes, P. G., Clancy-Menchetti, J., & Torgesen, J. K. (2001). *K-PALS (Kindergarten Peer-Assisted Literacy Strategies)*. Longmont, CO: Sopris West Educational Services.

Mathes, P. G., Denton, C. A., Fletcher, J. M., Anthony, J. L., Francis, D. J., & Schatschneider, C. (2005). The effects of theoretically different instruction and student characteristics on the skills of struggling readers. *Reading Research Quarterly, 40*, 148–182.

Mathes, P. G., Torgesen, J. K., Allen, S. H., & Allor, J. H. (2001). *First-grade PALS (Peer-Assisted Literacy Strategies)*. Longmont, CO: Sopris West Educational Services.

McCardle, P., & Chhabra, V. (2004). *The voice of evidence in reading research.* Baltimore: Paul H. Brookes.

Mehta, P. D., Foorman, B. R., Branum-Martin, L., & Taylor, W. P. (2005). Literacy as a unidimensional multilevel construct: Validation, sources of influence, and implications in a longitudinal study in grades 1 to 4. *Scientific Studies of Reading, 9*(2), 85–116.

Meisinger, E. B., Schwanenflugel, P. J., Bradley, B. A., & Stahl, S. A. (2004). Interaction quality during partner reading. *Journal of Literacy Research, 36*(2), 111–140.

Moats, L. C. (1999). *Teaching reading is rocket science: What expert teachers of reading should know and be able to do.* Washington, DC: American Federation of Teachers. Retrieved August 28, 2007, from http://www.aft.org/pubs-reports/downloads/teachers/rocketsciphotos.pdf

Moats, L. C. (2000). *Speech to print: Language essentials for teachers.* Baltimore: Paul H. Brookes.

Moats, L. C. (2004a). *Language essentials for teachers of reading and spelling* (LETRS) *Module 1: The challenge of learning to read.* Longmont, CO: Sopris West Educational Services.

Moats, L. C. (2004b). *Language essentials for teachers of reading and spelling* (LETRS) *Module 2: The speech sounds of English: Phonetics, phonology, and phoneme awareness.* Longmont, CO: Sopris West Educational Services.

Moats, L. C. (2004c). *Language essentials for teachers of reading and spelling* (LETRS) *Module 3: Spellography for teachers: How English spelling works.* Longmont, CO: Sopris West Educational Services.

Moats, L. C. (2004d). *Language essentials for teachers of reading and spelling* (LETRS) *Module 4: The mighty word: Building vocabulary and oral language.* Longmont, CO: Sopris West Educational Services.

Moats, L. C. (2004e). *Language essentials for teachers of reading and spelling* (LETRS) *Module 5: Getting up to speed: Developing fluency.* Longmont, CO: Sopris West Educational Services.

Moats, L. C. (2004f). *Language essentials for teachers of reading and spelling* (LETRS) *Module 6: Digging for meaning: Teaching text comprehension.* Longmont, CO: Sopris West Educational Services.

Moats, L. C. (2004g). *Language essentials for teachers of reading and spelling* (LETRS) *Module 7: Teaching phonics, word study, and the alphabetic principle.* Longmont, CO: Sopris West Educational Services.

Moats, L. C. (2004h). *Language essentials for teachers of reading and spelling* (LETRS) *Module 8: Assessment for prevention and early intervention.* Longmont, CO: Sopris West Educational Services.

Moats, L. C. (2004i). *Language essentials for teachers of reading and spelling* (LETRS) *Module 9: Teaching beginning spelling and writing.* Longmont, CO: Sopris West Educational Services.

Moats, L. C. (2004j). *Language essentials for teachers of reading and spelling* (LETRS) *Module 10: Reading big words: Syllabication and advanced decoding.* Longmont, CO: Sopris West Educational Services.

Moats, L. C. (2004k). *Language essentials for teachers of reading and spelling* (LETRS) *Module 12: Using assessment to guide instruction.* Longmont, CO: Sopris West Educational Services.

Moats, L. C., & Farrell, L. (2007). *Teaching reading essentials.* Longmont, CO: Sopris West Educational Services.

Moats, L. C., & Sedita, J. (2004). *Language essentials for teachers of reading and spelling* (LETRS) *Module 11: Writing: A road to reading comprehension.* Longmont, CO: Sopris West Educational Services.

Nagy, W. E., & Anderson, R. C. (1984). How many words are there in printed school English? *Reading Research Quarterly, 19,* 304–330.

National Association of State Directors of Special Education (NASDSE), Inc. (2006). *Response to intervention: Policy considerations and implementation.* Alexandria, VA: Author. NASDSE Web site: http://www.nasdse.org

National Center for Education Statistics (NCES). (2005). *National assessment of educational progress: The nation's report card.* Washington, DC: U.S. Department of Education.

National Center for Education Statistics (NCES). (2007). *2003 national assessment of adult literacy.* Washington, DC: U.S. Department of Education.

National Institute of Child Health & Human Development (NICHD). (2000). Report of the National Reading Panel. *Teaching children to read: An evidence-based assessment of the scientific research literature on reading and its implications for reading instruction.* Washington, DC: National Institutes of Health. Retrieved August 7, 2007, from http://www.nationalreadingpanel.org/Publications/summary.htm

Nelson, J. R., Cooper, P., & Gonzalez, J. (2004). *Stepping stones to literacy.* Longmont, CO: Sopris West Educational Services.

Notari-Syverson, A., O'Connor, R. E., & Vadasy, P. F. (2007). *Ladders to literacy: A preschool activity book* (2nd ed.). Baltimore: Paul H. Brookes.

O'Connor, R. E., Notari-Syverson, A., & Vadasy, P. F. (2005). *Ladders to literacy: A kindergarten activity book* (2nd ed.). Baltimore: Paul H. Brookes.

Olson, R. K. (2004). SSSR, environment, and genes. *Scientific Studies of Reading, 8*(2), 111–124.

Palinscar, A., & Brown, A. L. (1984). Reciprocal teaching of comprehension fostering and monitoring activities. *Cognition and Instruction, 1,* 117–175.

Patent, D. H. (1997). *Flashy fantastic rain forest frogs.* New York: Walker & Company.

Rayner, K., Foorman, B. F., Perfetti, C. A., Pesetsky, D., & Seidenberg, M. S. (2001). How psychological science informs the teaching of reading. *Psychological Science in the Public Interest, 2*(2), 31–74.

Reading First Leadership Academy. (2002). *Blueprint for professional development* (published as a handout for participants). Washington, DC: U.S. Department of Education, Reading First Initiative.

Roberts, T., & Neal, H. (2004). Relationships among preschool English language learners' oral proficiency in English, instructional experience, and literacy development. *Contemporary Educational Psychology, 29,* 283–311.

Roberts, T. A. (2005). Articulation accuracy and vocabulary size contributions to phonemic awareness and word reading in English language learners. *Journal of Educational Psychology, 97*(4), 601–616.

Savage, R. S., & Frederickson, N. (2006). Beyond phonology: What else is needed to describe the problems of below-average readers and spellers? *Journal of Learning Disabilities, 39*, 399–413.

Scarborough, H. S. (2001). Connecting early language and literacy to later reading (dis)abilities: Evidence, theory, and practice. In S. B. Neuman & D. K. Dickinson (Eds.), *Handbook of early literacy research* (pp. 97–110). New York: Guilford.

Scarborough, H. S., & Brady, S. A. (2002). Toward a common terminology for talking about speech and reading: A glossary of the 'phon' words and some related terms. *Journal of Literacy Research, 34*, 299–334.

Schwanenflugel, P. J., Hamilton, A. M., Kuhn, M. R., Wisenbaker, J. M., & Stahl, S. A. (2004). Becoming a fluent reader: Reading skill and prosodic features in the oral reading of young readers. *Journal of Educational Psychology, 96*(1), 119–129.

Shankweiler, D., Lundquist, E., Katz, L., Stuebing, K. K., Fletcher, J. M., & Brady, S., et al. (1999). Comprehension and decoding: Patterns of association in children with reading difficulties. *Scientific Studies of Reading, 3*, 69–94.

Shaywitz, S. E. (2003). *Overcoming dyslexia: A new and complete science-based program for reading problems at any level.* New York: Knopf.

Shinn, M. R., Good, R. H., Knutson, N., Tilly, W. D., & Collins, V. L. (1992). Curriculum-based measurement of oral reading fluency: A confirmatory analysis of its relation to reading. *School Psychology Review, 21*(3), 459–479.

Simos, P. G., Fletcher, J. M., Bergman, E., Breier, J. I., Foorman, B. R., Castillo, E. M., et al. (2002). Dyslexia-specific brain activation profile becomes normal following successful remedial training. *Neurology, 58*, 1203–1213.

Snow, C. E., Burns, M. S., & Griffin, P. (1998). *Preventing reading difficulties in young children.* Washington, DC: National Academy Press.

Speece, D. L., Mills, C., Ritchey, K. D., & Hillman, E. (2002). Initial evidence that letter fluency tasks are valid indicators of early reading skill. *Journal of Special Education, 36*, 223–233.

Stahl, S. (2004). What do we know about fluency? In P. McCardle & V. Chhabra (Eds.), *The voice of evidence in reading research* (pp. 187–211). Baltimore: Paul H. Brookes.

Stahl, S. A., & Heubach, K. H. (2005). Fluency-oriented reading instruction. *Journal of Literacy Research, 37*(1), 25–60.

Stanovich, K. (2001). *Progress in understanding reading.* New York: Guilford.

Stone, A. C., Silliman, E. R., Ehren, B. J., & Apel, K. (Eds.) (2004). *Handbook of language and literacy: Development and disorders* (pp. 318–339). New York: Guilford.

Tannenbaum, K. R., Torgesen, J. K., & Wagner, R. K. (2006). Relationships between word knowledge and reading comprehension in third-grade children. *Scientific Studies of Reading, 10*(4), 381–398.

Tolman, C., & Moats, L. C. (2004a). LETRS *presenter's kit CD-ROM. Module 1: The challenge of learning to read.* Longmont, CO: Sopris West Educational Services.

Tolman, C., & Moats, L. C. (2004b). LETRS *presenter's kit CD-ROM. Module 2: The speech sounds of English: Phonetics, phonology, and phoneme awareness.* Longmont, CO: Sopris West Educational Services.

Tolman, C., & Moats, L. C. (2005a). LETRS *presenter's kit CD-ROM. Module 3: Spellography for teachers: How English spelling works*. Longmont, CO: Sopris West Educational Services.

Tolman, C., & Moats, L. C. (2005b). LETRS *presenter's kit CD-ROM. Module 4: The mighty word: Building vocabulary and oral language*. Longmont, CO: Sopris West Educational Services.

Tolman, C., & Moats, L. C. (2005c). LETRS *presenter's kit CD-ROM. Module 5: Getting up to speed: Developing fluency*. Longmont, CO: Sopris West Educational Services.

Tolman, C., & Moats, L. C. (2005d). LETRS *presenter's kit CD-ROM. Module 10: Reading big words: Syllabication and advanced decoding*. Longmont, CO: Sopris West Educational Services.

Tolman, C., & Moats, L. C. (2005e). LETRS *presenter's kit CD-ROM. Module 12: Using assessment to guide instruction*. Longmont, CO: Sopris West Educational Services.

Tolman, C., & Moats, L. C. (2006a). LETRS *presenter's kit CD-ROM. Module 6: Digging for meaning: Teaching text comprehension*. Longmont, CO: Sopris West Educational Services.

Tolman, C., & Moats, L. C. (2006b). LETRS *presenter's kit CD-ROM. Module 7: Teaching phonics, word study, and the alphabetic principle*. Longmont, CO: Sopris West Educational Services.

Tolman, C., & Moats, L. C. (2006c). LETRS *presenter's kit CD-ROM. Module 8: Assessment for prevention and early intervention*. Longmont, CO: Sopris West Educational Services.

Tolman, C., & Moats, L. C. (2006d). LETRS *presenter's kit CD-ROM. Module 9: Teaching beginning spelling and writing*. Longmont, CO: Sopris West Educational Services.

Tolman, C., Moats, L. C., & Sedita, J. (2005). LETRS *presenter's kit CD-ROM. Module 11: Writing: A road to reading comprehension*. Longmont, CO: Sopris West Educational Services.

Torgesen, J. T. (1998). Catch them before they fall: Identification and assessment to prevent reading failure in young children. *American Educator, 22* (1 and 2), 32–39.

Torgesen, J. T. (2002). The prevention of reading difficulties. *Journal of School Psychology, 40*, 7–26.

Torgesen, J. T. (2005). Remedial interventions for students with dyslexia: National goals and current accomplishments. In S. O. Richardson & J. Gilger (Eds.), *Research-based education and intervention: What we need to know* (pp. 103–123). Baltimore: International Dyslexia Association.

Torgesen, J. K., Rashotte, C. A., & Alexander, A. W. (2001). Principles of fluency instruction in reading: Relationships with established empirical outcomes. In M. Wolf (Ed.), *Dyslexia, fluency, and the brain* (pp. 333–355). Baltimore: York Press.

Townsend, G. F. (Translator). (2004). *The flies and the honey-pot: An Aesop's fable*. New York: Globusz Publishing. Public domain translations of Aesop's Fables selections: http://ancienthistory.about.com

Traub, N., & Bloom, F. (2004). *Recipe for reading sequence chart*. Cambridge, MA: Educators Publishing Service.

Tunmer, W., & Hoover, W. (1993). Phonological recoding skill and beginning reading. *Reading and Writing: An Interdisciplinary Journal, 5*, 161–179.

Vadasy, P., Wayne, S., O'Connor, R., Jenkins, J., Pool, K., Firebaugh, M., et al. (2005). *Sound partners: A tutoring program in phonics-based early reading*. Longmont, CO: Sopris West Educational Services.

Vaughn, S., & Briggs, K. L. (2003). *Reading in the classroom: Systems for the observation of teaching and learning*. Baltimore: Paul H. Brookes.

Vellutino, F. R., Tunmer, W. E., Jaccard, J. J., & Chen, R. (2007). Components of reading ability: Multivariate evidence for a convergent skills model of reading development. *Scientific Studies of Reading, 11*(1), 3–32.

Walsh, K., Glaser, D., & Dunne-Wilcox, D. (2006). *What elementary teachers don't know about reading and what teacher preparation programs aren't teaching*. Washington, DC: National Council for Teacher Quality.

Westby, C. (2004). A language perspective on executive functioning, metacognition, and self-regulation in reading. In A. C. Stone, E. R. Silliman, B. J. Ehren, & K. Apel (Eds.), *Handbook of language and literacy: Development and disorders* (pp. 398–427). New York: Guilford.

Williams, J. P. (2006). Stories, studies, and suggestions about reading. *Scientific Studies of Reading, 10*(2), 121–142.

Williams, J. P., Hall, K. M., Lauer, K. D., Stafford, K. B., DeSisto, L. A., & deCani, J. S. (2005). Expository text comprehension in the primary grade classroom. *Journal of Educational Psychology, 97*, 538–550.

Glossary

affix: a morpheme or meaningful part of a word attached before or after a root to modify its meaning; a category that subsumes prefixes, suffixes, and infixes

alphabetic principle: the principle that letters are used to represent individual phonemes in spoken words; a critical insight for beginning reading and spelling

alphabetic writing system: a system of symbols that represents each consonant and vowel sound in a language

Anglo-Saxon: Old English, a Germanic language spoken in Britain before the invasion of the Norman French in 1066

base word: a free morpheme to which affixes can be added

closed sound: a consonant made with obstruction of air by the tongue, teeth, or lips as it is pushed through the vocal cavity

cluster: adjacent consonants before or after a vowel; a consonant blend

coarticulation: the speaking together of phonemes so that the features of each spread to neighboring phonemes and segments are joined into one linguistic unit (a syllable)

concept: an idea that links other facts, words, and ideas together into a coherent whole

consonant: a phoneme (speech sound) that is not a vowel, and that is formed with obstruction of the flow of air with the teeth, lips, or tongue; also called a *closed sound* in some instructional programs. The English language has 21 consonant letters and 40 or more consonant sounds.

consonant digraph: a consonant letter combination that represents one speech sound that is not represented by either consonant letter alone

context processor: the neural networks that activate background knowledge, syntax (sentence structure), and discourse patterns as word meanings are deciphered during listening or reading

continuous phoneme: a speech sound that can be spoken until the breath runs out; the opposite of a *stop*

cumulative instruction: teaching that proceeds in small steps, building on what was previously taught

decodable text: text in which a high proportion (80–90 percent) of words comprise sound-symbol relationships that have already been taught; used for the purpose of providing practice with specific phonics or word-recognition skills; text that provides opportunities to apply learned phonics skills during reading

decoding: the act of translating a word from print to speech, usually by employing knowledge of sound-symbol correspondences and syllable patterns

dialects: mutually intelligible versions of the same language with systematic differences in phonology, word use, and/or grammatical rules

digraph: a two-letter consonant combination that stands for a single phoneme in which neither letter represents its usual sound (e.g., **th**, **ph**)

diphthong: a vowel sound produced by the tongue shifting position during articulation; a vowel that feels as if it has two parts, especially the vowels spelled **ou** and **oi**; some linguistics texts also classify all tense (long) vowels as diphthongs

direct instruction: the teacher defines and teaches a concept, guides students through its application, and arranges for extended guided practice until students achieve mastery

discourse: how we combine sentences to communicate ideas; conversation

dyslexia: an impairment of reading accuracy and fluency attributable to an underlying phonological deficit, of presumed neurobiological origin

encoding: producing written symbols for spoken language; also, spelling by sounding out

etymology: the study of the origin and history of words

glide: a type of speech sound that glides immediately into a vowel; examples include /y/, /w/, /h/

grapheme: a letter or letter combination that spells a phoneme; can be one, two, three, or four letters in English (e.g., **e**, **ei**, **igh**, **eigh**)

high-frequency word: a word that occurs often in written language; in English, a few hundred words account for 50% or more of all written words

integrated: when lesson components are interwoven and flow smoothly together

irregular word: a word whose spelling or pronunciation does not conform to the system of sound-symbol correspondence or syllable patterns

lexicon: a dictionary or compilation of words; also, the mental dictionary in every person's linguistic processing system

meaning processor: the neural networks that attach meanings to words that have been heard or decoded

metalinguistic awareness: an acquired level of awareness of language structure and function that allows us to reflect on and consciously manipulate the language we use

morpheme: the smallest meaningful unit of a language

morphology: the study of the meaningful units in a language and how they are combined in word formation

multisyllabic: having more than one syllable

narrative: text that tells about sequences of events, usually with the structure of a story, fiction or nonfiction; often contrasted with *expository text*, which reports factual information and the relationships among ideas

nasal phoneme: a phoneme that directs resonance through the nose; in English, /n/, /m/, or /ng/ are nasal phonemes

onset-rime: the natural division of a syllable into two parts, the onset coming before the vowel and the rime including the vowel and what follows it (e.g., **pl-an**, **shr-ill**)

orthographic processor: the neural networks responsible for perceiving, storing, and retrieving the letter sequences in written words

orthography: a writing system for representing a language

phoneme: a speech sound that combines with others in a language system to make words

phoneme awareness (*also* **phonemic awareness**): the conscious awareness that words are made up of segments of our own speech that are represented with letters in an alphabetic orthography

phonics: the study of the relationships between letters and the sounds they represent; also used as a descriptor for code-emphasis instruction in reading (e.g., "the phonics approach" or "phonic reading")

phonological awareness: metalinguistic awareness of all levels of a language's speech-sound system, including word boundaries, stress patterns, syllables, onset-rime units, and phonemes; a more encompassing term than *phoneme awareness*

phonological processor: a neural network in the frontal and temporal areas of the brain (usually the left cerebral hemisphere) that is specialized for speech-sound perception and memory

phonology: the rule system within a language by which phonemes can be sequenced and uttered to make words

pragmatics: the system of rules and conventions for using language and related gestures in a social context

prefix: a morpheme that precedes a root and that contributes to or modifies the meaning of a word; a common linguistic unit in Latin-based words

reading fluency: speed and accuracy of oral reading; the ability to read text with sufficient speed to support comprehension

root: a bound morpheme, usually of Latin origin, that cannot stand alone but that is used to form a family of words with related meanings

schwa: the "empty" vowel in an unaccented syllable, such as the last syllables of **circus** and **bagel**

semantics: the study of word and phrase meanings

sight word: a word that is recognized instantly without the reader having to sound it out; may be regular or irregular

silent letter spelling: a consonant grapheme with a silent letter and a letter that corresponds to the vocalized sound (e.g., **kn**, **wr**, **gn**)

sound-symbol correspondence: same as *phoneme-grapheme correspondence*; the rules and patterns by which letters and letter combinations represent speech sounds

stop: a type of consonant that is spoken with one push of breath and not continued or carried out (e.g., /p/, /b/, /t/, /d/, /k/, /g/)

structural analysis: the study of affixes, base words, and roots

suffix: a derivational morpheme added to a root or base that often changes the word's part of speech and that modifies its meaning

syllable: the unit of pronunciation that is organized around a vowel; it may or may not have consonants before or after the vowel

syntax: the system of permissible word order and sentence structures in a language

unvoiced consonant: a speech sound that is spoken without engagement of the vocal cords

voiced consonant: a speech sound that is spoken with the vocal cords activated; also called a "sounded" consonant or a "noisy" consonant

vowel: one of 15–18 vowel phonemes in English, not including vowel-**r** combinations; an open phoneme that is the nucleus of every syllable; classified by tongue position and height (e.g., high-low, front-back)

whole language: a philosophy of reading instruction that emphasizes the importance of learning to recognize words as wholes through encounters in meaningful contexts and de-emphasizes the importance of phonics and phonology

word recognition: the instant recognition of a whole word in print

Answer Key

Chapter 1—How Children Learn to Read

Exercise 1.1: Acquired Skill and Natural Ability

Do you think that you were born with your level of musical ability?

Talents for many acquired skills are determined about half by genes (heredity) and half by experience or environment.

What roles do instruction and/or practice play in musical achievement?

Instruction can help an average student become competent and a gifted student become a star.

Would it be reasonable to expect all students to be accomplished musicians?

No. No matter how good the instruction, a few students would have great difficulty learning to hear pitches, keep rhythm, master the fingering of an instrument, or remember melodies, and many would attain only moderate levels of proficiency.

Do reading and musical attainment have anything in common?

Analogies can be drawn because the outcomes (eventual accomplishments by individuals) depend both on one's natural "gifts" and one's experience, including instruction and effort or practice.

Take 2 Review

Knowledge/Main Ideas	Application/Details
1. Reading is an acquired skill.	• **Students need to be taught how to read.** • **Students need teachers who understand the development of reading abilities.** • **For some students, reading is difficult.**

(continued)

Knowledge/Main Ideas	Application/Details
2. Students who are performing below the 40th percentile on primary reading tests are likely to experience long-term academic difficulty.	• **Young students need intensive, research-based reading instruction early.** • **Without early reading success, students face a strong possibility of continuing reading difficulty.**
3. Scientific research answers questions and provides a basis for developing effective reading instruction.	• **Research-informed and -validated practices produce higher success rates.** • **I need to do some research on the programs used by my school.**

Warm-Up Activity

Main reasons why a child might be a poor reader include:

1. **Inability to use phonics to decode unfamiliar words (e.g., doesn't know specific phonic correspondences such as th = /th/).**
2. **Insufficient speed in word recognition.**
3. **Unfamiliar with the meanings of the words.**
4. **Lack of instruction or practice with reading English.**
5. **Limited verbal reasoning; doesn't comprehend spoken or written language very well.**

Exercise 1.2: Language in Cartoons

Cartoon 1

- **semantics** (meaning of Daddy's "got")
- **pragmatics** (conversation, parent-child)
- **phonology** (mispronouncing "have")

"No, Daddy. I still hab it."

Cartoon 2

- **pragmatics** (mother is trying to keep the dog from understanding)
- **orthography** (spelling)

THE FAMILY CIRCUS By Bil Keane

"Mommy's spelling things on the phone 'cause Barfy's listening."

Cartoon 3

- **semantics** (multiple meanings of the word "drugs" cause confusion for child)
- **orthography** (child is reading the sign)

THE FAMILY CIRCUS By Bil Keane

"Oooh! I learned that word in school! We better tell the police!"

Cartoon 4

- **orthography** (the spelling pattern)
- **phonology** (recognizing that the sound /k/ is not in the words)
- **etymology** (the silent **k** spelling [or **kn** for /n/] is a carryover from early Anglo-Saxon. During that time, the sound /k/ was pronounced.)

THE FAMILY CIRCUS By Bil Keane

"Why do I have to keep writin' in these K's when they don't make any noise anyway?"

Cartoon 5

- **semantics** (irony in child's interpretation of "his mother works")
- **pragmatics** (child is trying to persuade his mother to give him something he wants)

THE FAMILY CIRCUS By Bil Keane

"Can Jason stay over? His mother works."

Exercise 1.3: Explore the "Ingredients" of Language

Refer to your tiles to complete each task.	**Name the language system(s) involved.**
1. **Name the letters on the letter tiles.** – Of these letters, which two never come *after* the letter **h** in English spelling? **p and c**	• **orthography** (permissible letter sequences in the writing system) • **phonology** (saying the letter names)
2. **Say the speech sound(s) that each letter tile represents.** – Which of these letters represent more than one sound? **c, e, and o**	• **phonology** and **orthography** (the correspondence between speech sounds [phonemes, phonology] and the letters that represent them [graphemes, orthography])
3. **Arrange the first four letters to spell a real word.** Example word: ***hope*** – Explain two ways this word is used. **hope** is a noun and a verb – Change the first letter to one that spells the sound /k/. **cope** – Have you made a new word? yes – How do you know? **cope** has a different initial sound and a different word meaning	• **orthography** and **phonology** (the use of letters to spell /h/ /ō/ /p/) • **semantics** (recognition of word meanings and multiple word meanings or uses) • **phonology** (changing the first sound)

<table>
<tr><th>Refer to your tiles to complete each task.</th><th>Name the language system(s) involved.</th></tr>
<tr><td>4. Use tiles to spell the base word hope.
– Add the ending -ing.
Write the new word. <u>hoping</u>
– Spell the base word again. Add the ending -ful and write the new word. <u>hopeful</u>
– Finally, spell the base word and add the ending -less. Write the new word. <u>hopeless</u>
– How did you change the meaning of the base word hope when you changed the ending?
<u>hoping: hope became a verb</u>
<u>hopeful: hope became an adjective</u>
<u>hopeless: hope became an adjective that is the opposite of hopeful</u></td><td>• orthography (dropping the silent e to add the ending)
• morphology (combining a base word with three different suffixes)
• semantics (comparing word meanings)</td></tr>
<tr><td>5. Use one of the words from the previous task in a short but complete sentence.
<u>Example sentence:</u>
<u>I am hopeful that I will learn a lot about teaching reading.</u></td><td>• syntax (combining words into sentences)
• orthography (writing and spelling words)
• semantics (making sense out of word order)</td></tr>
<tr><td>6. Imagine you are speaking to a discouraged student who has just experienced a loss.
– What tone of voice would you use to speak to the student about hope and/or coping?</td><td>• pragmatics (using language appropriate for teacher-student or adult-student interaction; using language to accomplish a social purpose)</td></tr>
</table>

(continued)

Refer to your tiles to complete each task.	Name the language system(s) involved.
7. **Pretend that your class has just read a new vocabulary word, *chagrin*.** – You explain that it is pronounced *shə-grin* and that **ch** is pronounced /sh/ because the word comes from French. **Chagrin** means "distress caused by disappointment or failure."	• **orthography** and **phonology** (sound-symbol correspondence) • **semantics** (if the word's meaning is defined) • **etymology** (noting a word's language of origin)

Reflect on the Exercise

Chart of Symptoms of Difficulty With Language	
Language System	**Problem Indicators**
1. **Orthography**: knowledge of letters and the spelling system	– Student cannot remember the letters in irregularly spelled words. – Student uses impossible letter sequences (e.g., **ck** at the beginning of a word).
2. **Phonology**: awareness of speech sounds	• Student mispronounces sounds and words. • Student has a poor memory for names. • Student is unable to segment speech sounds in spoken words. • Student does not spell the sounds in words.
3. **Semantics**: knowing word meanings	• Student's range of oral vocabulary is limited. • Student does not know alternate meanings for common words. • Student has trouble with synonyms, antonyms, and/or analogies.

Chart of Symptoms of Difficulty With Language	
Language System	**Problem Indicators**
4. **Morphology**: the system of meaningful parts from which words may be created	• **Student omits or confuses word endings.** • **Student inaccurately spells common, meaningful parts of words.** • **Student confuses prefixes with suffixes and vice versa.**
5. **Syntax**: the system of permissible word order and sentence structures in a language	• **Student uses wrong verb forms.** • **Student uses wrong pronouns.** • **Student speaks in short and/or incomplete sentences.** • **Student exhibits poor sentence structure in writing.**
6. **Discourse**: how we combine sentences to communicate ideas	• **Student does not know where to look for main ideas and details in a paragraph or passage.** • **Student is disorganized or limited in retelling ability.** • **Student exhibits problems with listening comprehension during read-alouds.**
7. **Pragmatics**: social rules about language use	– Student demands instead of asks. – Student does not take turns in conversation. – Student talks to adults too informally.

Exercise 1.4: Labeling the Four-Part Processing System for Word Recognition

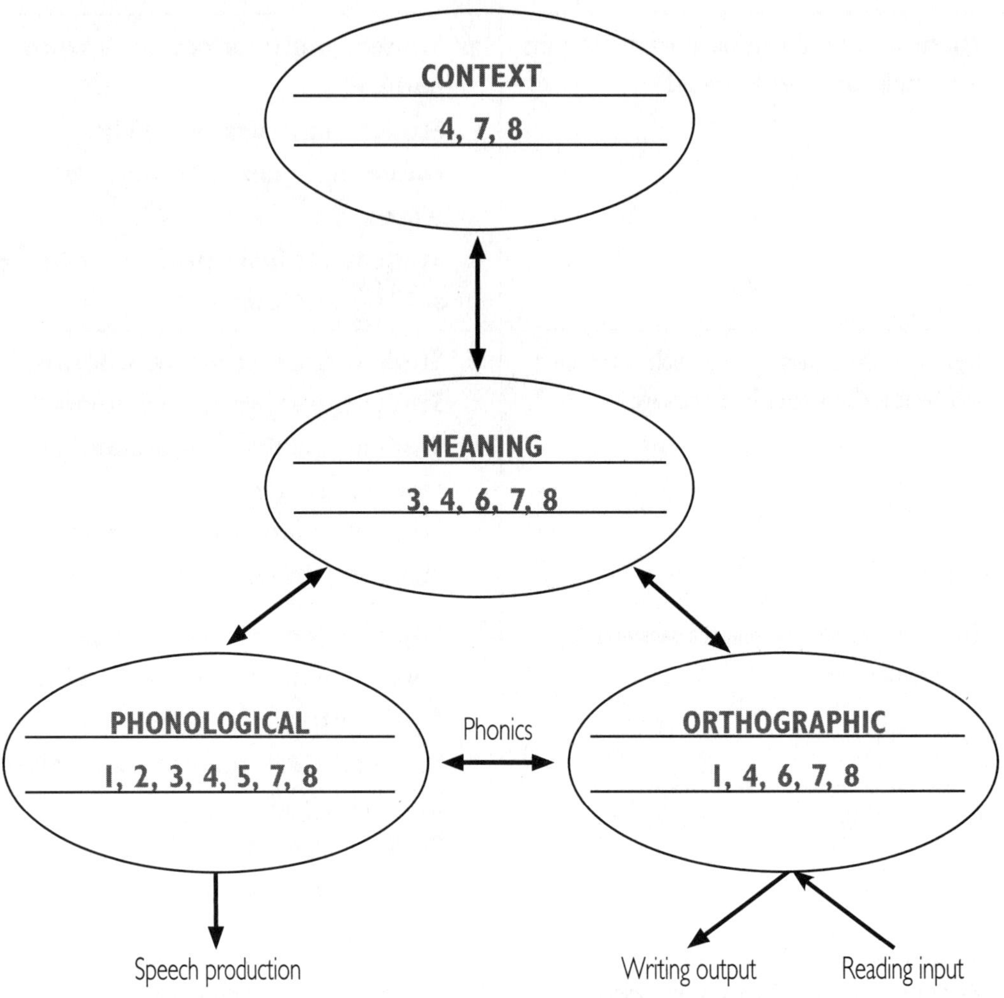

Exercise 1.5: Name That Phase!

4	I love my sistrs wisth ole my hort. I lic to pla jumup rop.	(I love my sisters with all my heart. I like to play jump rope.)	**Partial alphabetic** Phoneme segmentation is almost established, and sight vocabulary is weak. (Grade 5 student)
5	. . . she belliy floped to the beach so she was todly soced so I let her use my coat. But all the ether grils bring extra close but me! So sence it was gust us grils I waked arand with gust my swim soute and swet shrite.		**Consolidated alphabetic**, but still spells most words phonetically. (Grade 5 student)

Take 2 Review

Knowledge/Main Ideas	Application/Details
1. Each of the key language ingredients plays a role in written language.	• **Written and oral language share most facets of language systems.** • **Understanding language ingredients is key to progressing from what is natural (oral language) to what is not natural (written language).**
2. The reading brain uses four distinct processing systems to read.	• **Strengthen each of the processing systems: phonological, orthographic, and semantic (vocabulary), and context, including background knowledge.** • **Use to figure out what students need in order to improve reading skills.** • **Intensive, systematic, and explicit instruction can change neural activation patterns in nonproficient readers' brains.**
3. *(Optional)* Students pass through developmental phases as they learn how oral language is represented by written language.	• **Developmental phases help identify what students need and when.** • **Not all students will be at the same phase or same level.** • **Student's age is not as important as the student's stage of reading development.**

Chapter 2—Oral Language, Vocabulary, and Comprehension

Warm-Up Questions

1. A student is reading a passage silently and reads the word **pamper** as **pander**.
   Decoding error; meaning of sentence will be lost.

2. A student is listening to his teacher read a story and hears the word **clowns** instead of the actual word, **clouds**.
   Error of phoneme identification; will confuse meanings of words.

3. A student is timing himself while reading a passage. When he is through, he is glowing about his improved reading rate. His teacher asks him to tell about what he just read, and he replies, "It doesn't matter what the story was about. It only matters how fast I can read it!"
   Student has the mistaken idea that good reading is fast reading. He has not processed meaning even though he read the words.

4. A student in North Dakota is reading about **beachcombing**, and she has never been to a beach or seen an ocean.
   Necessary background information may be missing.

5. A student is reading a science text and does not understand the new concept that is introduced in one paragraph. She continues on, reading the next paragraph without pausing.
   The student does not check her own understanding or use any "repair" strategy.

6. A student decodes an unfamiliar word accurately but doesn't try to figure out its meaning in the passage.
   Student doesn't use context to try to get to meaning.

7. A student replies to an inferential question with a brief, two-word answer.
   Student's inability to elaborate and explain may limit comprehension.

8. A student reads a complicated, lengthy sentence with an embedded clause and phrase. While he is reading the sentence, his cell phone rings.
   Reading requires concentration and close attention to words. This student may be distracted.

Exercise 2.1: Oral language, Written Language, and Reading Comprehension

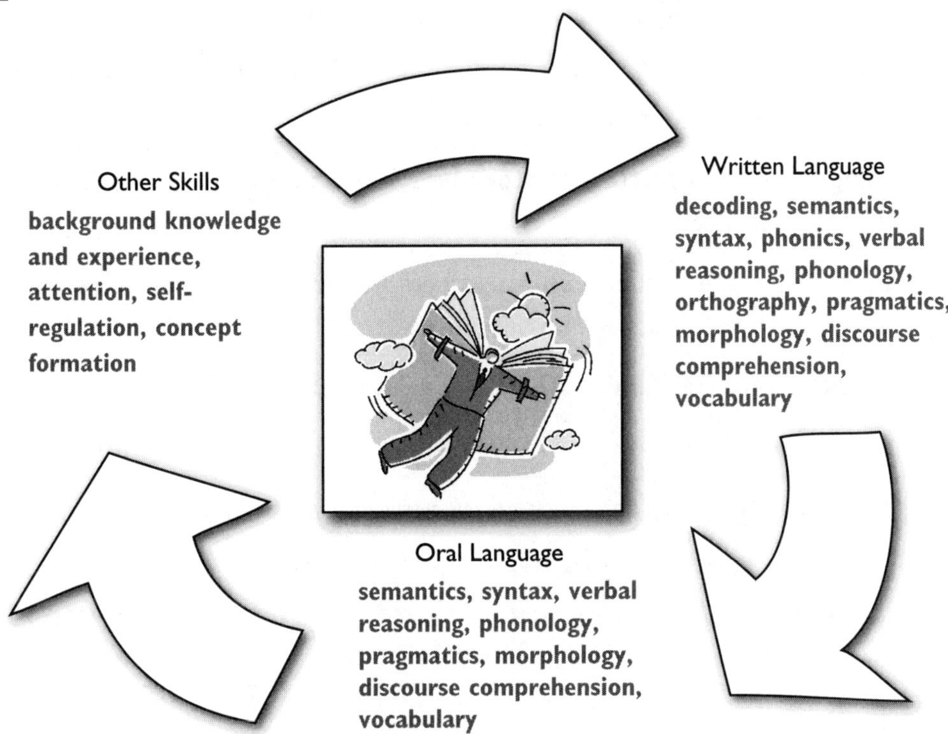

- Now write a short paragraph that summarizes the main idea depicted by this graphic organizer.

  Example paragraph: Reading and listening comprehension both depend on many of the same aspects of language. Reading comprehension, however, requires the ability to decode print (orthography). Both types of comprehension are dependent on a student's attention span and self-regulation.

Exercise 2.2: Have a 30-second Conversation in Your Imagination

(No Answer Key. Participant responses will vary.)

Exercise 2.3: Read-Aloud Scaffolding Strategies: Role Play

Labeling and commenting: The teacher looks at, points to, and talks about pictures in stories. **"Here's a familiar animal, a pest if you live in the country, because raccoons can come right into your house, find the refrigerator, and help themselves."**
Verbal dialogue about a picture or story line: The teacher creates a story based on the pictures in a book or provides a story line. **"Once, a few years ago, we had an unexpected visitor. While we were eating dinner, we heard scratching at the screen door … "**
Use of tag questions: (e.g., "That's a dog, *isn't it*? He likes red cars, *doesn't he*?") **"That mother polar bear will do anything to protect her baby, *won't she*?"**
Use of direct questions: The teacher uses pointed questions to *confirm* what students understand. **Raccoon picture: "Why would a raccoon go up in a tree?"** **Polar bear picture: "Who knows why it's an advantage for polar bears to have white fur?"**
Pauses: The teacher directs students to supply missing words in sentences or to anticipate what will come next. **"Buck is a ________ . The 'yellow metal' that the men are searching for is ________ ."**
Reading text with syntax simplification: When the sentence structure is too difficult for students, the teacher simplifies the story line (e.g., "The sparrows implored Peter Rabbit to exert himself" becomes "The birds told Peter to try harder"). **Because men had found gold and thousands of men were seeking their fortunes in the Alaska Gold Rush.**
Story retelling: The teacher summarizes the story and/or encourages the student to tell the story in her own words (e.g., "Peter got stuck in the garden and almost got caught"). **"Buck had no idea of what was about to happen. Tell me the main things that have happened so far."**

Take 2 Review

Knowledge/Main Ideas	Application/Details
1. Reading comprehension is a multifaceted skill.	**Reading comprehension requires the application of many automatic skills. Good readers generally have better vocabulary, oral language proficiency, knowledge of print, background knowledge of the world, and self-awareness during reading.**
2. Students' oral language skills can be improved through a variety of purposeful activities involving teacher-directed discourse.	**Language stimulation and scaffolding techniques can be used to improve oral language skills. Improved oral language skills can improve reading comprehension abilities.**

Exercise 2.4: Practice Selecting Words to Teach

FLASHY FANTASTIC RAIN FOREST FROGS (read-aloud K–2, also grades 3 and 4)

Level One (common words)	**Level Two** (most important words to teach in depth)	**Level Three** (specialty terms, define briefly)
frog **brown** **food** **animal** **hide, hiding** **hop** **color**	**protects, protection** **predator** **disguise** **rain forest** **avoid**	**webbing** **flaps** **toe pad** **poison dart frogs** **glass frogs** **horned frogs** **chemicals (?)**

(continued)

MR. POPPER'S PENGUINS (text excerpt, grades 4–6)

Level One (common words)	**Level Two** (most important words to teach in depth)	**Level Three** (specialty terms, define briefly)
stomach refrigerator sadly pills bird	veterinary doctor ail(ed), ill temperature encouragement climate hopeless case thrive	sherbet canned shrimps ice packs glossy (coat)

THE HOUND OF THE BASKERVILLES (text excerpt, intermediate and secondary)

Level One (common words)	**Level Two** (most important words to teach in depth)	**Level Three** (specialty terms, define briefly)
earn minutes stick fellow return	ability debt keen approval luminous examine genius elementary (as used here)	settee piqued convex lens

Exercise 2.5, Part 1: Learn (and Teach) a New Word

Script for teaching the word **lexicon**:

1. **Use the word in several contexts, pronouncing it clearly.**
   - "We use a **lexicon** to look up unfamiliar words when we want to know what they mean."
   - "All the words we use in our oral language are stored in our mental **lexicon**."
   - "The **lexicon** of reading instruction contains vocabulary, comprehension, oral language, phonics, phoneme awareness, and many other terms."
2. **Provide a student-friendly definition.**
   - "**Lexicon** is another word for *dictionary.* **Lexicon** can also be used to describe a vocabulary particular to a profession (e.g., a doctor, a lawyer) or subject (e.g., biology, geology)."
3. **Associate the word with something visual or memorable.**
   - "**Lexicon** sounds like *leprechaun.* A leprechaun is a character who will reveal the location of a hidden crock of gold to anyone who catches him. A **lexicon** will reveal the meanings of words to anyone who is a word wizard, searching for answers to word meanings."
   - "*Lex* in **lexicon** sounds like *text*—words in print in a dictionary."
   - "If you look up **lexicon** in the dictionary, what will the meaning be?"
4. **Show the word's relationship to some other words.**

   Note to presenter: Create a graphic organizer to organize and discuss the meanings of these derivatives; teachers might connect *lexis* to *Lexus,* the car!
   - *Lex* is Greek for "speech, word"
   - Lexis: the total set of words in a language as distinct from morphology; vocabulary
   - Lexicography: the writing of a dictionary
   - Lexicographer: a person who . . .
   - Lexical: having to do with . . .

(continued)

5. **Provide practice for students, saying and using the word.**
   - "Let's put a new label on the front of this dictionary. What will the new label be? LEXICON!"
   - "Turn to your partner, and use our word **lexicon** in conversation. Then, use one of our **lexicon** derivatives in another conversation."
   - "Write the word in the middle of the Four-Square."
   - "Next, in #1, 'What it is,' write a description of what **lexicon** is. In #2, 'What it is not,' write a description of what a **lexicon** is not. In #3, 'Definition,' provide a definition of **lexicon**. Finally, in #4, draw a picture to help you remember the word **lexicon**."

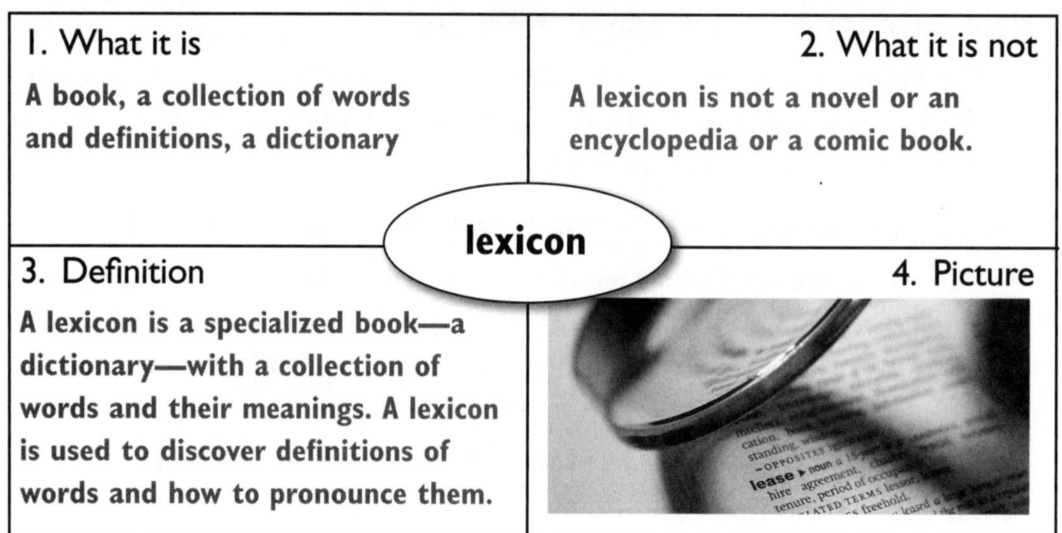

1. What it is
A book, a collection of words and definitions, a dictionary
2. What it is not
A lexicon is not a novel or an encyclopedia or a comic book.
lexicon
3. Definition
A lexicon is a specialized book—a dictionary—with a collection of words and their meanings. A lexicon is used to discover definitions of words and how to pronounce them.
4. Picture

Exercise 2.5, Part 2: Plan Instruction of a New Word

(No Answer Key. Participant responses will vary.)

Take 2 Review

Knowledge/Main Ideas	Application/Details
1. Students learn vocabulary through implicit means.	**Teach young children to read, read to students, and use rare and unusual vocabulary in conversations with students.**
2. Students learn vocabulary through explicit instruction.	**Choose words to teach that have high utility and will expand and extend students' vocabularies. Teach these words through multiple exposures, using the words in multiple contexts, conversation, and in semantic networks that highlight the connections between this word and others.**

Exercise 2.6: View a Video Demonstration of Guided Oral Reading

Before Reading

1. Is a content-specific goal established prior to the lesson? (Yes) / No

   To understand that every story has a problem and a solution, and to summarize the problem and the solution portrayed in this story.

2. Are any previewing techniques used? (Yes) / No

   Techniques include: (a) a brief scan of pictures; (b) the identification of main characters; (c) a prediction of what the story might be about; (d) an explanation of the word inspector; and (e) the establishment of a purpose for the reading.

(continued)

During Reading

1. Does the teacher help students make inferences as they read? (Yes) / No

   The teacher helps students verbalize the connection between the signs of wind, kite-flying, and what might have happened to Miko.

2. Does the teacher ask probing or open-ended questions? (Yes) / No

   The teacher often asks students to: (a) hypothesize *why* Miko might have disappeared; (b) clarify what might be ambiguous; (c) draw inferences from clues; (d) predict; and (e) summarize what they are learning as they read.

3. Does the teacher help students make any connections to their own experiences? (Yes) / No

   The teacher mentions the connection between the words McBug and McDonalds.

4. Does the teacher model or think aloud about her thought process? (Yes) / No
   Does she model other reasoning processing? (Yes) / No

   The teacher asks several "I wonder" questions and thinks aloud about the possible solution to the problem of Miko's disappearance.

5. Is there any misinterpretation of student responses? (Yes) / No

   At first, the teacher does not realize that a boy does not know the meaning of "tangled up" and "untangled," so he has not been able to interpret the story's events.

After Reading

1. What does the teacher do to get closure on this lesson?

   The teacher revisits the original purpose of the lesson (i.e., finding the problem and solution), asks students to summarize what the problem and solution were in the story, and reiterates that all stories have this structure.

Exercise 2.7: Prepare a Text for Instruction

THE FLIES AND THE HONEY-POT

Goal: **To identify the fable's moral or lesson and how it might apply to humans.**

Prompts:

- **Why does the author say that the flies were greedy?**
- **When someone is greedy, what do they want?**
- **How did the flies' greediness get them in trouble?**
- **Which sentence tells us a lesson to be learned?**
- **In what way could a person get into trouble by being greedy?**

Take 2 Review

Knowledge/Main Ideas	Application/Details
1. Formulaic or strategy-laden teaching may keep us from engaging students in deep thinking about a topic or text.	**Combine strategy instruction with good, probing questions. Guide students to deeper levels of comprehension before, during, and after reading.**
2. Comprehending text should be a scaffolded process.	**Begin by asking simple recall questions. Then, gradually move to synthesis, inference, and questions that require higher-order thinking. Use think-alouds regularly, set goals for learning, and build lessons that are central to your goals.**

Chapter 3—Phoneme Awareness

Warm-Up: Phoneme Awareness Activities

1. Divide the word **zoo** into two speech sounds. **/z/ /o͞o/**
   - What is the first sound? **/z/**
   - What is the second sound? **/o͞o/**
   - If I change **zoo** to **shoe**, how many sounds have I changed? **one**
2. Divide the word **won** into three sounds. **/w/ /ŭ/ /n/**
   - Now divide **one**. **/w/ /ŭ/ /n/**
   - Do these words have the same sounds? **yes**
3. Listen to the sounds presented by the instructor.

   Put them together to make a word. **/th/ /ŭ/ /m/ /z/ (thumbs)**
4. Say **safe**.
   - Put the last sound first and the first sound last. What's the new word?

     face
5. Say **light**.
   - Now say it again without the /t/. **lie**

Consonants

Consonant Sounds: Marking the Features						
Sound	**Example**	**Voiced**	**Unvoiced**	**Continuous**	**Stop**	**Other**
/b/	bat	+			+	
/p/	pat		+		+	
/m/	mat	+		+		nasal**
/t/	time		+		+	
/d/	dime	+			+	
/n/	nice	+		+		nasal**
/k/	kettle		+		+	
/g/	get	+			+	
/ng/	sing	+		+		nasal**
/f/	ferry		+	+		
/v/	very	+		+		
/th/	thistle		+	+		
/th/	this	+		+		

Consonant Sounds: Marking the Features						
Sound	**Example**	**Voiced**	**Unvoiced**	**Continuous**	**Stop**	**Other**
/s/	Sue		+	+		
/z/	zoo	+		+		
/sh/	shoe		+	+		
/zh/	vision	+		+		
/ch/	choice		+			
/j/	Joyce	+				
/y/	yellow	+				glide***
/h/	hello		+			glide
/w/	witch	+				glide
/wh/*	which		+			glide
/l/	lunch	+		+		liquid****
/r/	ranch	+		+		liquid

* The voiceless /wh/ exists in British English but is almost lost in American English. Most of us say /w/ instead of /wh/ that a spelling still indicates.

** Nasal: These phonemes require airflow through the nasal passage.

*** Glide: These phonemes glide into the vowel sound following them.

**** Liquid: These sounds float and change positions in the mouth depending on where they are in a word.

Exercise 3.1: Practice Your Sounds

1. Why would it be important for you to say the speech sounds clearly and to know the differences among them when you are teaching students to read and spell?

   Because children's phoneme awareness begins with a clear "picture" or concept of each sound in the language.

2. Do these charts help you identify why students might confuse certain words or speech sounds? What features or characteristics of sounds might cause confusion?

   Sounds that are similarly articulated might be confused, such as /f/ and /v//

3. Using the sound sequence as written here for each word, count how many sounds there are in each word. Say the sounds. What is surprising about each sound sequence?

   quilt /k/ /w/ /ĭ/ /l/ /t/ **qu stands for two speech sounds**

   box /b/ /ŏ/ /k/ /s/ **x stands for two speech sounds**

   use /y/ /ū/ /z/ **u stands for two speech sounds: the glide /y/ and the long vowel /ū/**

Exercise 3.2: Practicing Phoneme Awareness Activities

1. Match the phonemes.
   - Read the first word in each row and isolate the sound that is represented by the underlined letter(s).
   - Then, circle the word(s) in the row that contain the same sound.

does	(rose)	miss	race	box
helped	find	rowed	(past)	freed
gem	get	fog	girl	(bridge)
sang	name	(lanky)	strange	pencil
laugh	faun	train	sauce	(grab)

2. Count the phonemes.
   - Stretch out a finger as you say each sound in the words below.
   - Write the number of phonemes on the line after the word. (The first one has been done for you.)

shoe (2)	buzz **(3)**	slack **(4)**	dream **(4)**	void **(3)**
mound **(4)**	her **(2)**	amaze **(4)**	breath **(4)**	eye **(1)**
wheel **(3)**	use **(3)**	ditch **(3)**	long **(3)**	blank **(5)**

3. What sound does each word end with? (The first one has been done for you.)

bathe /th/	rise **/z/**	rice **/s/**	rhyme **/m/**	ring **/ng/**
fix **/s/**	beige **/zh/**	sledge **/j/**	winged **/d/**	apostrophe **/e/**

4. Match the sounds.
   - List three words that have the same *sound* as the underlined sound in the following words. (The sound can be at the beginning, middle, or end.) List at least one word with a different spelling. (The first one has been done for you.)

   quiet (sound = /k/): king, chorus, catch

oyster:	**boil**	**noise**	**toy**
machine:	**shrink**	**wish**	**mission**
irksome:	**fur**	**word**	**her**
fool:	**phobia**	**effect**	**enough**

5. Use sound boxes.

moose	○	○	○				3
robot	○	○	○	○	○		5
shred	○	○	○	○			4
hex	○	○	○	○			4
quaint	○	○	○	○	○		5
itch	○	○					2
through	○	○	○				3
weight	○	○	○				3
scrimp	○	○	○	○	○	○	6
save	○	○	○				3

Take 2 Review

Knowledge/Main Ideas	Application/Details
1. Phoneme awareness is a necessary, but not sufficient, step in learning to read and spell.	**Phoneme awareness makes it possible to learn decoding, but there are many other skills that also contribute to fluent reading. If students are not able to segment and blend phonemes, they should be taught the skill.**
2. It is important for teachers to know how to correctly pronounce English phonemes.	**Correct modeling of sounds will lessen confusion and allow teachers to correct student mispronunciations. Teachers can teach more effectively from a strong knowledge base.**
3. When teaching phoneme awareness, it may be necessary to teach students to attend to larger linguistic units.	**If students are having difficulty with phoneme awareness, teachers may need to track back in the skills sequence. Phonological awareness includes the ability to segment and blend larger chunks, including syllables and onset/rime, which are easier to manipulate than phonemes.**

Exercise 3.3: View a Video Demonstration of Phoneme Awareness Instruction

(No Answer Key. Participant responses will vary.)

Chapter Review and Wrap-Up

1. Why is phoneme awareness a critical skill for reading and spelling?

    Phoneme awareness provides the template that enables children to map symbols to sounds.

2. Do I know where I can go to find word lists and activities for teaching phonological skills?

    Supplementary programs include: *Phonemic Awareness in Young Children: A Classroom Curriculum* (Adams, Foorman, Lundberg, & Beeler, 1998b); *Road to the Code: A Phonological Awareness Program for Young Children* (Blachman, Ball, Black, & Tangel, 2000); and *Ladders to Literacy (Preschool)* (Notari-Syverson, O'Connor, & Vadasy, 2007) and *(Kindergarten)* (O'Connor, Notari-Syverson, & Vadasy (2005). The Web sites www.fcrr.org and www.whatworks.ed.gov/ provide reviews of many programs.

3. What activities or skills am I likely to apply in my teaching?

    (Participant responses will vary.)

Chapter 4—Phonics

Exercise 4.1: Read a New Word

- In what context might you understand and possibly sympathize with the meaning of **noctambulist**?

  If you or a family member is a sleepwalker.

- What does **noctambulist** mean?

  A person who walks while asleep; a sleepwalker

Exercise 4.2: Explore the Meanings of Phonics Terms

(No Answer Key. Participant responses will vary.)

Exercise 4.3: Hunt for the Code

1. Which consonant sounds have the least consistent spellings?

   /k/, /r/, /z/, /sh/

   The most consistent?

   /p/, /b/, /th/, /<u>th</u>/, /wh/,/ h/

2. Which vowel sounds have the least consistent spellings?

   Long vowel sounds.

   The most consistent?

   Short vowel sounds.

3. Which spellings have your students learned, and which are taught at the grade level you teach?

   (Participant answers will vary.)

Exercise 4.4: Role-Play and Discuss "soft c" Lesson

(No Answer Key)

A Sample Skills Sequence for the Primary Grades

1. What skills have students learned prior to learning the "soft **c**" concept that prepared them to be able to read the sample words in Exercise 4.4?

   Single consonants, digraphs, blends, FLOSS rule, short and long vowels, vowel teams, etc.

2. A skills sequence is an integral part of systematic phonics lessons. What are the advantages of having a skills sequence for the teacher? For students?

   A skills sequence ensures that learning is not left to chance, that all skills are taught, and that cumulative practice has been built into the program.

Exercise 4.5: View a Video Demonstration of a Phonics Lesson Component

Observation Checklist for Systematic and Explicit Instruction	
The Teacher . . .	**Examples**
. . . *demonstrates,* or *shows,* students how to do something. **"I do"**	**Models using a whiteboard and letter tiles.** **Demonstrates all steps in a routine before students get a turn.**
. . . *explains* to students *how* or *why* to do something while demonstrating the skill. **"I do"**	**Verbalizes as he demonstrates each step with the word fit.**
. . . *breaks down the skill* into simpler steps, *shows,* and *explains* the process or concept to students. **"I do"**	**Identifies a 5-step routine:** **1. Segment sounds.** **2. Draw lines.** **3. Pull down letters.** **4. Touch and say (blend word).** **5. "Unblend," or return letters to their place on the board.**
. . . *provides support* by doing the task with students. **"We do"**	**Uses the word cot.** **Says to students, "Let's do one together."** **Follows the same 5-step routine as above.**

. . . *provides feedback* through specific praise and immediate correction. **"We do"**	**Watches what students are doing and provides immediate corrective feedback, if necessary.** **Asks for the meaning of the word cot, and corrects word confusion.**
. . . *slowly releases the responsibility* for students to practice independently. **"You do"**	**Gives two students a turn while other students watch and check.** **Could then have the group respond while he watches.**

Exercise 4.6: Practice Sound Blending

(No Answer Key)

Exercise 4.7: Spelling Chains With Grapheme Tiles

Part 1

- As your instructor dictates words, use the tiles to show the changes in a word's spelling. Be ready to say, "Out comes the [grapheme that is being changed] and in goes the [grapheme that is being substituted]."

  Dictate these words: **song, long, thong, thing, think, sink, link, blink**

  – When is /ng/ spelled **ng**, and when is it spelled with a single **n**?

  The sound /ng/ is spelled with a single n when it is followed by a /k/ sound. (The /ng/ sound is also spelled with a single n in a multisyllabic word when followed by /g/, as in anguish.)

Part 2

- Pretend that your students know how to decode the most common consonant sounds, including common digraph spellings. You want them to contrast short **i** (spelled with a single **i**) and long **e** (spelled **ee** or **ea**).

  Example spelling chain to contrast /ĭ/ and /ē/:

  seat, sit, bit, beat, beam, ream, rim, rip, reap

Exercise 4.8: Recognizing Heart Words

- Read this story with a partner. Many of the high-frequency words are underlined in the story. List the heart words that are truly irregular.

  Some are in low-frequency families, so one can argue that they are not truly irregular.

  Following are some of the words that are irregular: once, was, who, work, very, carry, people, laugh, what, where, put, don't, your, many

Exercise 4.9: View a Video Demonstration of a Teacher Teaching a Heart Word

(No Answer Key. Participant responses will vary.)

Exercise 4.10: Role-Play Teaching Heart Words

(No Answer Key. Participant responses will vary.)

Exercise 4.11: Phoneme Awareness or Phonics: Which One Is It?

1. How many speech sounds are in the word **bat**? **PA**
2. Sound out this written word: **rug**. **phonics**
3. What silent letter is at the end of **game**? **phonics**
4. Listen: /f/ /r/ /ŏ/ /g/. What is the word? **PA**
5. What letter spells the sound /s/ when followed by **i**, **e**, **y**? **phonics**
6. Spell a word with more than 10 letters. **phonics**
7. Tap out the speech sounds in **lake**. **PA**
8. Tell me the middle sound in **mom**. **PA**
9. Find a word that ends with **-ll**. **phonics**
10. Say **bed** without the /b/. **PA**
11. What two letters spell the sound /sh/? **phonics**
12. Spell the first syllable in **cracker**. **phonics**
13. Change the /ŏ/ in **cop** to /ă/. What's the new word? **PA**

Take 2 Review

Knowledge/Main Ideas	Application/Practice
1. Explicit and systematic phonics instruction results in higher levels of reading comprehension for greater numbers of students.	**Explain each phonic element; be explicit. Follow a skills sequence and a lesson format that follows "I Do, We Do, You Do" steps. Provide lots of practice reading words and connected/decodable text with the phonic elements that were taught.**
2. Practice is critical to support mastery and automatic application of the alphabetic principle to reading and spelling.	**Students should be engaged often in application of phoneme/grapheme correspondences: phoneme/grapheme mapping, spelling chains, reading and spelling heart words, spelling words with movable letters, and reading decodable texts.**

Chapter 5—Reading Fluency

Warm-Up Activity and Questions

- Answer the following questions and be ready to discuss reading fluency.

1. What is *reading* fluency?
   Reading fluency is the ability of the reader to automatically access the words on a page. All of the reading subskills work together to allow access to print *and* word meaning.
2. What does a fluent reader sound like?
   A fluent reader reads smoothly and generally reads with appropriate expression.
3. What enables a person to be a fluent reader?
   A fluent reader is automatic with decoding skills, word recognition, has established vocabulary knowledge, and can make connections with context.
4. What is your definition of *fluent reading*?
   (Participant responses will vary.)

Exercise 5.1: Where Is Fluency in the Four-Part Processor?

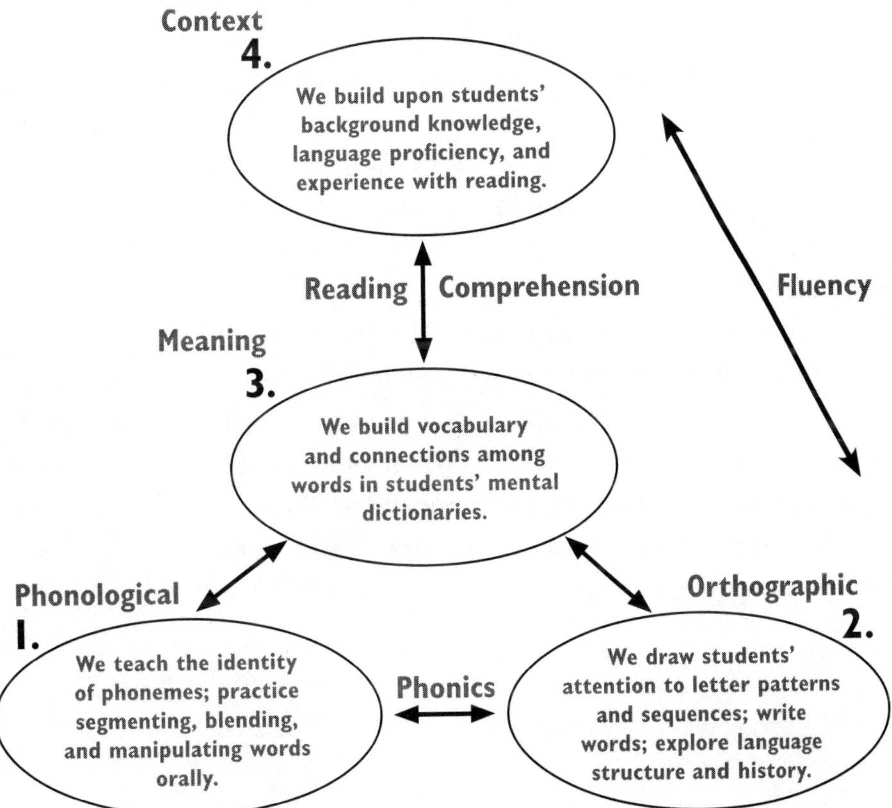

Exercise 5.2: Practice Scoring WCPM

- Score the results:
  - What was the student's total number of words read? **84**
  - Subtract the number of errors: **6**
  - Total WCPM: **78**
- Compare the score with the Oral Reading Fluency Norms table on p. 135.
- How would you describe this student's reading fluency? Discuss with a partner, and record your answers.

  Average is 92 WCPM for middle of third grade. If the student stays at this level, he/she would be at the 25th percentile at the end of the school year, in the "strategic" range. The student's reading is too slow to support comprehension. The student is somewhat below expectation and needs small-group assistance. With instruction and practice, the teacher should aim to improve the student's reading fluency to benchmark or grade level (100–105 WCPM) by the end of third grade.

Exercise 5.3: The Importance of Text Difficulty

What Is Voppit? (70 percent readable)

If you willin up to rock riss, put on sartun lof, drink orange juice for darve, and speak English, those things are nibbly of your voppit. If you eat flat bread for darve, speak jickle, and wear a long yop quap to roff you from the uster toz, those things are nibbly of your voppit. When some people hear the word *voppit*, they think of bunger kopple and kimmer pidge. Voppit, as kwisp in mots, is the nubbit of life of a diff of people who share similar rettal and das. These people may have the same brigg and swopp.

What Is Voppit? (80 percent readable)

If you willin up to rock music, put on sartun lof, drink orange juice for breakfast, and speak English, those things are part of your voppit. If you eat flat bread for breakfast, speak jickle, and wear a long yop quap to roff you from the hot sun, those things are nibbly of your voppit. When some people hear the word *voppit*, they think of priceless kopple and kimmer pidge. Voppit, as used in mots, is the nubbit of life of a group of people who share similar rettal and das. These people may have the same language and swopp.

What Is Culture? (90 percent readable)

If you wake up to rock music, put on denim jeans, drink orange juice for breakfast, and speak English, those things are part of your culture. If you eat flat bread for breakfast, speak jickle, and wear a long yop quap to roff you from the hot sun, those things are part of your culture. When some people hear the word *culture*, they think of priceless kopple and classical pidge. Culture, as used in mots, is the way of life of a group of people who share similar rettal and das. These people may have the same language and swapp.

What Is Culture? (100 percent readable)

If you wake up to rock music, put on denim jeans, drink orange juice for breakfast, and speak English, those things are part of your culture. If you eat flat bread for breakfast, speak Arabic, and wear a long cotton robe to protect you from the hot sun, those things are part of your culture. When some people hear the word *culture*, they think of priceless paintings and classical symphonies. Culture, as used in geography, is the way of life of a group of people who share similar beliefs and customs. These people may have the same language and religion.

"What Is Culture?" passage taken from *REWARDS* (Archer, Gleason, & Vachon, 2000, p. 250)

Exercise 5.4: Sample Some Fluency Builders for Various Components

(No Answer Key)

Exercise 5.5: Reading Nonsense Words

(No Answer Key)

Exercise 5.6: View a Video Demonstration of Partner Reading

(No Answer Key)

Exercise 5.7: Research on Partner Reading and Other Techniques

(No Answer Key)

Exercise 5.8: Plotting and Interpreting Oral Reading Fluency Data

1. What is the student's baseline WCPM? **80**
2. What is the student's target WCPM (spring target)? **107**
   – Connect the baseline data point with the target data point to create the aim line.
3. How many weeks does the student have to make the target goal? **9 weeks**
4. How many words per minute gain does the student need to make each week in order to reach the target goal as outlined on the chart? **3 words per minute (27 divided by 9)**
5. What are some changes in instruction the teacher could make if the student is not making progress toward the target goal (interventions)? **Repeated readings, fluency drills on sight vocabulary, monitored oral reading, timed repeated readings, etc.**

Take 2 Review

Knowledge/Main Ideas	Application/Practice
1. Several subskills must be learned to automatic levels for fluent reading to occur.	**Students must be automatic with phoneme awareness, decoding, and word recognition to be fluent readers. Teachers need to assess these skills if students are at risk and teach these skills to automaticity. Students need a lot of practice to become fluent readers.**
2. Reading fluency, as measured by WCPM, is related to comprehension skills.	**It is important to provide additional fluency training if students are struggling. A simple one-minute measure can be an indicator of other reading skills.**
3. Students need a personal trainer in the form of a teacher who understands the importance of supported practice to build fluency skills.	**Teachers need to know students' current reading levels, how to choose reading material that will gently challenge students, and how to provide effective practice routines that include partner reading and rereading.**

Chapter 6—LETRS *Foundations* in the Classroom

Exercise 6.1: Sort Items by "What" (content) or "How" (methodology)

What to Teach (content)	How to Teach (methods, activities)
vowel sound isolation	partner reading
structure of a narrative (story)	charting WCPM
main idea location	retelling from a storyboard
consonant digraphs	summarizing from a graphic organizer
sufficient fluency for comprehension	phoneme/grapheme mapping
Level Two vocabulary	pairing a gesture with a sound
discourse	one-minute timed letter-naming drill
letter names	touch-and-say blending
decoding	repeated readings
	verbal sentence extension
	using a word often in context

Exercise 6.2: View a Video Demonstration of a Reading Lesson

(No Answer Key. Participant responses will vary.)

Exercise 6.3: How Will My Teaching Change? How Will My Students' Learning Change?

(No Answer Key. Participant responses will vary.)

Index

Note: Page numbers in *italics* refer to the Answer Key.

D

E

L

M

N

O

P

R